Euchologium Anglicanum

EUCHOLOGIUM ANGLICANUM

Prayers of Christian Faith and Practice'

by

JOHN E. W. WALLIS
Sometime Scholar of Brasenose College, Oxford,
Late Canon of Lichfield

AND LESLIE M. STYLER
Fellow and Chaplain of Brasenose College

with Latin versions by

F. C. GEARY
Emeritus Fellow of Corpus Christi College, Oxford

WIPF & STOCK · Eugene, Oregon

Wipf and Stock Publishers
199 W 8th Ave, Suite 3
Eugene, OR 97401

Euchologium Anglicanum
Prayers of Christian Faith and Practice
By Wallis, John W. and Styler, Leslie M.
Copyright©1963 SPCK
ISBN 13: 978-1-4982-8427-1
Publication date 6/22/2016
Previously published by SPCK, 1963

CONTENTS

FOREWORD	vii
PRAYERS FOR THE CHRISTIAN YEAR	
Sundays in Advent	4
Christmas Day	10
St Stephen	10
St John the Evangelist	12
Holy Innocents	12
Circumcision	14
Epiphany	14
Sundays after Epiphany	16
Conversion of St Paul	22
Little Lent	22
Ash Wednesday	26
Sundays in Lent	26
Maundy Thursday	32
Good Friday	36
Easter Even	38
Easter Day	40
Sundays after Easter	40
Ascension Day	46
Sunday after Ascension	46
Whitsun Eve	48

Whitsunday	48
Trinity Sunday	50
Sundays after Trinity	50

GROUPS OF PRAYERS

Sundays in Advent	82
New Year	110
Epiphany	118
Little Lent	126
Trinity	130

APPENDIXES

1. The Cursus in Latin and English	137
2. Traditional Endings of Collects	140

FOREWORD

This is a collection of prayers, projected but unhappily not completed, by the late John Eyre Winstanley Wallis, sometime Scholar of Brasenose College, Oxford, Canon and Chancellor of Lichfield Cathedral. "I composed them from time to time", he said, "for use after the Third Collect at Sunday Evensong in the Cathedral, with a congregation often consisting largely of visitors who had come to see the building, and only incidentally to join in our worship, i.e. more or less casual visitors, not specifically devout churchpeople. It seemed to me that the early Sacramentaries supplied the very models that I wanted, Christian but not technical. I set to work first to translate prayers from these, but I was driven in time to write prayers. So I have gradually got together a considerable number of prayers which have at any rate been 'tried out' (if one may use such a word about prayers) for rhythm and audibility, and for appositeness of material."

The series was intended to follow the Christian year, with one prayer for each Sunday and Holy Day, based on the credal sequence from Advent to Trinity Sunday, and on "Faith in Practice" for the Sundays after Trinity. In addition there were to be Groups

of prayers for various occasions or seasons, such as Epiphanytide and "Little Lent", these latter "not so terse as the Sunday prayers, enabling us to explore more in detail the devotional field of a subject". There are thirty such prayers in the collection.

At the beginning of 1957 Canon Wallis proposed to me that I should provide Latin versions to accompany the originals, which he thought might enhance their interest and value. "The ultimate aim" he said, "for the English version is a prayer that the Vicar will use in the prayers after the Third Collect, clear, short, audible, and easily enunciated to fill the Church; the Latin, on the other hand, will be used mainly by the Vicar and his educated laity at their prayer desks, where the work of engaging the mind with the heart in its devotions is very greatly assisted by the use of Latin. . . . If the work is blessed, we shall be putting into the hands of Christian persons a book which may be of comfort and help to them in their devotional life and worship, and one that I hope might be used as a supplement to the authorised prayers of public worship."

The composition of the English prayers was based, as suggested above, on the language and rhythms of the early Sacramentaries, which from long study were familiar to him. A note on the rules of the Latin accentual Cursus, which have been followed in the translations, may be found in the Appendix on page 140.

At the time of Canon Wallis's death in September

1957 the Sunday series had been carried from Advent to Trinity Sunday. I have been extremely fortunate in persuading the Rev. Leslie Styler, the Chaplain of Canon Wallis's own College of Brasenose (to whose inspection and criticism we had at an early stage decided to submit the Collection), to provide the English prayers for the Sundays after Trinity, in order to complete the series for the whole year.

I am glad to record my grateful thanks to Mr Styler for his valuable and ready help, and to other friends whose encouragement and generosity have made the publication of this book possible. We venture to hope that this book may serve as a fitting memorial to a sincere and learned Christian priest, and fulfil in some measure the purpose he had in mind.

F.C.G.

Prayers for
The Christian Year

ADVENT SUNDAY

Let us pray for God's governance of our hearts.

V. Jesus Christ was a minister of the circumcision for the truth of God:
R. To confirm the promises made unto the fathers.
Rom. 15.8.

O Lord God, Holy Father, who hast revealed thyself through Jesus Christ by sending him to take man upon himself and to open the kingdom of heaven to those who believe on him:

So govern and direct our hearts, we beseech thee, that we may overcome all worldly temptations and live in continual readiness for his coming to judgement; through the same

ADVENT II

Let us pray for grace to learn what the Bible teaches us about God.

V. Whatsoever things were written aforetime:
R. Were written for our learning. *Rom.* 15.4.

O Eternal Father, who in time past hast revealed thy will to thy people through thy servants the prophets,

ADVENT SUNDAY

Oremus Deum ut corda nostra gubernet.

V. Jesus Christus minister fuit circumcisionis propter veritatem Dei:
R. Ad confirmandas promissiones patrum. *Rom.* 15.8.

Domine Deus, Sancte Pater, qui teipsum per Jesum Christum revelavisti, quoniam missus est ut hominem assumeret, et credentibus regnum aperiret caelorum:

Corda nostra, quaesumus, ita guberna et dirige, ut saeculares omnes superemus tentationes, et parati semper exspectemus dum iterum Judex mundi adveniat; per eundem

ADVENT II

Gratiam rogemus ut ea discamus quae de Deo in sacris scripturis docemur.

V. Quaecumque scripta sunt in principio:
R. Ad nostram doctrinam scripta sunt.   *Rom.* 15.4.

Pater sempiterne, qui in praeteritis saeculis per servos tuos prophetas voluntatem tuam hominibus revelasti,

and didst inspire apostles and evangelists to record for us Christ's work of salvation:

We humbly thank thee for the heritage which is ours in the Bible, for the eagerness of the preachers who have delivered thy message, for the historians' truthfulness, and for the zeal of those who have written of salvation in Jesus; give us grace to perceive the lessons which thou wouldest have us learn from the scriptures, so that when we read of thy power we may be encouraged, and comforted by the certainty of thy protection and mercy; through the same

ADVENT III

Let us pray for the Ministry of the Church.

V. The God of hope fill you with all joy and peace in believing:
R. That ye may abound in hope through the power of the Holy Ghost.   *Rom.* 15.13.

O God, whose Son our Saviour entrusted to his Apostles the ministry whereby thy saving truth is spread abroad amongst all men:

We beseech thee continually to pour upon thy Church the blessings of thy great mercy; enable thy ministers faithfully to publish the Gospel, and by their lives to show forth the power set free by his advent, and finally grant that all men may be drawn

qui gratiam apostolis et evangelistis dedisti ut Christi Salvatoris opus nobis describerent:

Gratias tibi humiliter agimus pro sacris scripturis quas nobis hereditatem dedisti, pro eorum studio qui tua verba nuntiaverunt, pro veritate scriptorum, pro diligentia omnium qui Jesum Salvatorem praedicaverunt; concede, quaesumus, ut sacrae scripturae doctrinam secundum voluntatem tuam ita discamus, ut in operibus tuis cognoscendis firmati spe certissima defensionis tuae et misericordiae confortemur; per eundem

ADVENT III

Oremus pro Sanctae Ecclesiae ministerio.

V. Deus spei repleat vos omni gaudio et pace in credendo:
R. Ut abundetis in spe et virtute Spiritus Sancti.

Rom. 15.13.

Domine Deus, cujus Filius Salvator noster ministerium apostolis suis mandavit, quo salutaris tua veritas inter omnes gentes diffunditur:

Effunde, quaesumus, super Ecclesiam tuam beneficia magnae tuae misericordiae; ministris ejus da potestatem ut evangelium fideliter praedicent, et vivendo potentiam adventu ejus liberatam demon-

to thee in faith, love, and repentance; through the same

ADVENT IV

Let us pray for grace to receive the message of Christmas.

V. My hands also will I lift up unto thy commandments, which I have loved:
R. And my study shall be in thy statutes. *Ps.* 119.48.

O gracious and merciful Father, who hast sent thy blessed Son into thy creation of time and space, and extendest thy love to all men:

We thank thee for thy tender care for us in sending us thy only-begotten Son Jesus Christ; we thank thee for the power which thou hast given us to receive his revelation that thou art our Father, and that by thy providence we have been brought out of the darkness of terror and ignorance into the clear light of the assurance of thy loving protection: and we beseech thee to continue to us thy blessing, that we may ever love and serve thee in joyful devotion; through the same

strent; et concede ut omnes homines in fide, affectu, poenitentia ad te adducantur; per eundem

ADVENT IV

Gratiam rogemus ut annuntiationem Nativitatis Domini accipiamus.

V. Levavi manus meas ad mandata tua quae dilexi:
R. Et exercebar in justificationibus tuis.   *Ps.* 118.48.[1]

Pater misericors, qui Filium tuum benedictum in mundum misisti, et omnes homines diligis:

Gratias tibi agimus qui pro sollicitudine tua nobis Filium tuum Unigenitum Jesum Christum misisti; benedicimus tibi quia per ejus revelationem te Patrem esse nostrum percepimus, et nos providentia tua de tenebris timoris et ignorantiae in lumen tuae tutelae esse vocatos; et benedictionem tuam perpetuam petimus, ut tibi semper pietate et affectu laeti deserviamus; per eundem

[1] The numbering of the Latin psalms throughout follows that of the Vulgate.

CHRISTMAS DAY

V. Glory to God in the highest:
R. And in earth peace to men of good will.
Luke 2.14.

O God, eternal Father, with whom in the beginning was Christ the Word who made all things:

We humbly thank thee for the birth of Jesus Christ at Bethlehem; and we beseech thee to give us grace by thy Holy Spirit to receive him with joy as the true light of the world, and faithfully to believe on his Name, that through the power which he gives us we may become thy sons and see his great glory; through the same

ST STEPHEN

V. I see the heavens opened:
R. And the Son of man standing on the right hand of God. *Acts* 7.56.

O Eternal and everlasting God, who didst accept and bless the witness of thy first martyr Saint Stephen, and didst grant him the vision of thy heavenly glory:

We humbly beseech thee by the grace of the Holy Spirit to give us strength in every trial of soul and body to remain stedfast in the faith, and to exalt the praise of thy holy Name; through

CHRISTMAS DAY

V. Gloria in altissimis Deo:
R. Et in terra pax hominibus bonae voluntatis.
Luc. 2.14.

Deus, sempiterne Pater, quocum in principio erat Christus Verbum, qui omnia fecit:

Tibi humiliter gratias agimus, quia Jesus Christus in Bethlehem natus est; et oramus te ut per gratiam Sancti tui Spiritus veram mundi lucem Filium tuum laeti accipiamus, et nomini ejus credentes et per ejus potentiam filii tui facti magnam ejus gloriam videamus; per eundem

ST STEPHEN

V. Ecce video caelos apertos:
R. Et Filium hominis stantem a dextris Dei.
Act 7.56.

Sempiterne Deus, qui cum tua benedictione Sancti Stephani Protomartyris testimonium accepisti, et visionem ei caelestis tuae gloriae revelasti:

Humiliter te obsecramus ut per Sancti Spiritus gratiam in omnibus et corporis et animae probationibus confirmemur, et in fide intenti laudem sancti tui nominis exaltemus; per

ST JOHN THE EVANGELIST

V. This is my commandment:
R. That ye love one another. *John* 16.12.

O Lord God, whose blessed apostle Saint John bade his disciples love one another:

Give us boldness of heart to love the Lord Jesus as he would be loved, and loving him to love also all those whom he loves; through the same

HOLY INNOCENTS

V. Out of the mouths of babes and sucklings:
R. Hast thou ordained strength, O Lord. *Ps.* 8.2.

O God, heavenly Father, who dost allot to each whom thou callest into existence his day, be it short or long, and his purpose:

Mercifully remember the child martyrs of Bethlehem; and grant that the witness which they bore by their deaths to the Incarnation of thy Son may not have been in vain, but may ever strengthen and increase the faith of thy servants; through the same

ST JOHN THE EVANGELIST

V. Hoc est praeceptum meum:
R. Ut diligatis invicem. *Joan.* 16.12.

Domine Deus, cujus dilectus apostolus Sanctus Joannes discipulis suis praecepit ut alterutrum diligerent:

Da nobis, quaesumus, fiduciam ut Dominum Jesum sicut ipse vult diligi diligamus, et eodem affectu omnes quos diligit amplectamur; per eundem

HOLY INNOCENTS

V. Ex ore infantium et lactentium:
R. Perfecisti laudem, Domine. *Ps.* 8.2.

Deus, Pater caelestis, qui eorum quos genuisti suum cuique spatium vitae, seu breve seu longum, et suum propositum tribuis:

Recordare, quaesumus, clementer martyrum infantium in Bethlehem occisorum; et concede ne inane Filii tui incarnationis testimonium dederint, sed ut eorum causa fides famulorum tuorum corroboretur semper et augeatur; per eundem

THE CIRCUMCISION

V. Submit yourselves to every ordinance of man:
R. For the Lord's sake. 1 *Pet.* 2.13.

O Lord God, whose blessed Son was by thy appointment subject to the ceremonial law of thy people:

Give us grace to reverence thy holy Church, and gladly to hear and obey its instruction; that being named with a Christian name, and signed with the sign of the Cross, we may fight resolutely all the days of our life as his soldiers in unceasing warfare against sin and wickedness; through the same

THE EPIPHANY

V. O sing unto the Lord a new song:
R. Sing unto the Lord, all the whole earth.
Ps. 96.1.

O God, eternal Father, who by thy gracious providence hast revealed to the gentiles the way of salvation:

Grant that we may day by day trust in the power of thy love thus made known to us in Christ Jesus; and so accomplish the perilous journey of this life, that at the last by thy great mercy we may enter into the unending joy of thy heavenly presence; through the same

THE CIRCUMCISION

V. Subjecti estote omni humanae creaturae:
R. Propter Dominum.   1 *Pet.* 2.13.

Domine Deus, qui Filium tuum benedictum populi tui ritibus subjici voluisti:

Da nobis gratiam ut sanctam tuam ecclesiam veneremur, et doctrinae ejus libenter obediamus; ut nos, Christi nomine nominati et signo crucis signati, sicut milites ejus constanter in omnibus vitae nostrae diebus contra peccatum et malitiam decertemus; per eundem

THE EPIPHANY

V. Cantate Domino canticum novum:
R. Cantate Domino omnis terra.   *Ps.* 95.1.

Deus, Pater sempiterne, qui ex providentia tua misericordi viam salutis gentibus revelasti:

Concede ut nos affectus tui potentiae sic in Jesu Christo revelatae quotidie confidamus; et ita per hujus vitae pericula proficiscamur, ut tandem per clementiam tuam in caelorum gaudia sempiterna intremus; per eundem

EPIPHANY I

V. I was glad when they said unto me:
R. We will go into the house of the Lord. *Ps.* 122.1.

O Eternal Lord God, whose blessed Son Jesus Christ when a child on earth was found sitting among the doctors in the Temple, both hearing them and asking them questions:

Grant that thy children may learn the things that are for their souls' health, and may daily grow in strength in thy service and favour; through the same

EPIPHANY II

V. With thee is the well of life:
R. And in thy light shall we see light. *Ps.* 36.9.

O Almighty and everlasting God, whose beloved Son for the replenishing of the wedding feast at Cana of Galilee turned water into wine, and manifested his authority over creation:

Grant, we pray thee, that as by thy inspiration men of science make discovery of natural powers till now unknown to us, we may devote these powers which are thine solely to thy glory and the welfare of thy people; through the same

EPIPHANY I

V. Laetatus sum in his quae dicta sunt mihi:
R. In domum Domini ibimus. *Ps.* 121.1.

Sempiterne Domine Deus, cuius Filium benedictum Jesum Christum etiam infantem in templo invenerunt parentes, in medio doctorum sedentem, ut audiebat eos et interrogabat:

Praesta, quaesumus, ut tui infantes, quicquid animis est salutare discentes, in servitium et gratiam tuam quotidie crescant et confortentur; per eundem

EPIPHANY II

V. Apud te est fons vitae:
R. Et in lumine tuo videbimus lumen. *Ps.* 35.10.

Omnipotens sempiterne Deus, cujus Filius dilectus, ad nuptias in Cana Galilaeae vocatus, aquam in vinum mutando se omnis creaturae potestatem habere monstravit:

Praesta, quaesumus, ut quoniam homines ingeniosi te inspirante rerum naturam explorant, et ignotas adhuc potestates acquirunt, nos eas ad tuam solum gloriam et populi tui beneficium dedicare possimus; per eundem

EPIPHANY III

V. Like as the hart desireth the water-brooks:
R. So longeth my soul after thee, O God.   *Ps.* 42.1.

O Almighty and everlasting God, who hast made known through Jesus Christ thy care for the outcast and stranger:

We humbly beseech thee to fill our hearts with love towards those who are cut off and isolated from the fellowship of thy servants, and grant that as messengers of thy power we may proclaim to the hopeless and lonely the companionship and comfort of the knowledge of Jesus; through the same

EPIPHANY IV

V. O be thou our help in trouble:
R. For vain is the help of man.   *Ps.* 60.11.

Almighty and eternal God, as of the seen so also Lord of the unseen:

Mercifully grant that our souls may never be possessed by the evil powers of estrangement and hatred; and give us grace in thy loving providence to make known in singleness of heart and mind the great things thou hast done for us; through

EPIPHANY III

V. Quemadmodum desiderat cervus ad fontes aquarum:
R. Ita desiderat anima mea ad te, Deus.   *Ps.* 41.1.

Omnipotens sempiterne Deus, qui per Jesum Christum te profugis et desolatis condolere significasti:

Te obsecramus ut cordibus nostris misericordiam infundas ad eos diligendos qui a famulorum tuorum excluduntur societate; praesta ut tuam praedicando potentiam miseros et desperantes societate et solacio in scientia Jesu perfrui doceamus; per eundem

EPIPHANY IV

V. Da nobis auxilium de tribulatione:
R. Quia vana salus hominis.   *Ps.* 59.13.

Omnipotens sempiterne Deus, qui eorum quae non videntur sicut eorum quae videntur es Dominus:

Adjuva nos clementer, ne unquam animae nostrae invidia et odio quasi daemoniis infestentur; et concede per affectum et providentiam tuam ut beneficia maxima quae nobis dedisti simpliciter omnibus praedicemus; per

EPIPHANY V

V. Blessed is the man that feareth the Lord:
R. He hath great delight in his commandments.

Ps. 112.1.

Almighty everlasting God, who hast entrusted the furtherance of thy purpose for the nations of the world to the goodwill of thy servants:

We humbly beseech thee to grant that all men may rejoice in the revelation of thy love in Jesus Christ, and seek diligently to promote and keep the peace of thy kingdom; through

EPIPHANY VI

V. O visit me with thy salvation:
R. That I may see the felicity of thy chosen.

Ps. 106.4-5.

O God, heavenly Father, who by thy Son hast made all things in heaven and earth, and yet desirest to draw to thyself our uncompelled love and devotion:

Grant us grace to understand the manifestation of thy Son as Christ the Lord and Saviour of mankind, and to engage all our affections in thy service, and labour to spread the Gospel among those who know him not; that when he shall come again in great glory he may find a people gladly awaiting his kingdom; through the same

EPIPHANY V

V. Beatus vir qui timet Dominum:
R. In mandatis ejus volet nimis. *Ps.* 111.1.

Omnipotens sempiterne Deus, qui famulorum tuorum voluntati committis ut quod omnibus terrae gentibus destinasti proficiant:

Humiliter obsecramus te ut omnes homines affectum tuum amoris in Christo Jesu revelatum laeti percipiant, et regni pacem tui prosequi studeant et servare; per

EPIPHANY VI

V. Visita nos in salutari tuo:
R. Ad videndum in bonitate electorum tuorum.
Ps. 105.4-5.

Deus, Pater caelestis, qui per Filium tuum caelestia omnia et terrestria creavisti, et tamen amorem nostrum injussum et pietatem desideras:

Da nobis gratiam ut intelligamus revelatum esse Filium tuum qui Christus Dominus et Salvator hominum esset, et sensibus nostris omnibus ad tuum servitium usi, evangelium inter ignorantes eum ita diffundere studeamus, ut tandem cum in gloria magna redierit, famulos suos regem exspectantes inveniat; per eundem

CONVERSION OF ST PAUL

V. My strength will I ascribe unto thee:
R. For thou art the God of my refuge. *Ps.* 59.9.

Almighty and eternal God, who didst send Saint Paul as thy apostle to the Gentiles, preaching the Gospel to all who would hear him:

Enable us, we humbly beseech thee, faithfully to believe that through Christ crucified and risen from the dead all men may be saved and brought into thy kingdom, there to rejoice in eternal life with him who liveth

LITTLE LENT

SEPTUAGESIMA: CREATION

V. Let them praise the name of the Lord:
R. For he commanded, and they were created.

Ps. 148.5.

Almighty and eternal God, who hast created us and all the world for thy pleasure and glory:

Grant us grace joyfully to accomplish that for which thou hast given us abundance of life in Christ Jesus, and help us gladly to obey thy will in the true freedom of service and the triumphant strength of obedience; through the same

CONVERSION OF ST PAUL

V. Fortitudinem meam ad te custodiam:
R. Quia, Deus, susceptor meus es. *Ps.* 58.10.

Omnipotens sempiterne Deus, qui Sanctum Paulum apostolum tuum ad gentes misisti, ut eis qui vellent audire evangelium praedicaret:

Adjuva nos, quaesumus, ut credamus fideliter omnes homines per Christum crucifixum et vivificatum salvari posse, et in regnum tuum induci, ubi aeterna vita cum eo laeti fruantur, qui tecum

LITTLE LENT

SEPTUAGESIMA: CREATION

V. Laudent nomen Domini:
R. Quia ipse mandavit et creata sunt. *Ps.* 148.5.

Omnipotens sempiterne Dens, qui nos et mundum totum in tuam ipsius delectationem et gloriam creavisti:

Praesta ut ea, ad quae facienda plenitatem nobis vitae in Jesu Christo dedisti, laetis mentibus exsequamur; adjuva nos ut libertate vera in serviendo, in obediendo certa firmitate aucti, voluntati tuae libenter obtemperemus; per eundem

SEXAGESIMA: REDEMPTION

V. My lips shall greatly rejoice when I sing unto thee:
R. And my soul, which thou hast redeemed.

Ps. 71.23.

Eternal and everlasting God, who didst so love the world as to send thy blessed Son to redeem us from sin and death:

Grant, we beseech thee, that we may accept with joyful hearts the consequences of this thy great love for mankind, and betake ourselves in humble thankfulness to the way of salvation which has been won for us by Jesus Christ our Redeemer and Saviour, who liveth

QUINQUAGESIMA: SANCTIFICATION

V. God hath chosen you to salvation:
R. Through sanctification of the Spirit.

2 *Thess.* 2.13.

Almighty everlasting God, whose Holy Spirit continually dwells with sanctifying power in the souls of the faithful:

Grant us grace to use his manifold gifts in thy service; make us wise with true wisdom, thoughtful through understanding, courageous in strength, informed by true knowledge, well founded in godliness, and reverent in adoring love; help us thus provided to rejoice with all thy people in our creation, redemption,

SEXAGESIMA: REDEMPTION

V. Exsultabunt labia mea cum cantavero tibi:
R. Et anima mea quam redemisti. *Ps.* 70.23.

Sempiterne Deus, qui mundum sic dilexisti ut Filium tuum mitteres benedictum, qui nos ab errore et morte redimeret:

Praesta, quaesumus, ut tanti affectus tui fructum laeti percipientes, et gratiam submisse agentes, in viam salutis progrediamur, ducente Jesu Christo Redemptore nostro et Salvatore; Qui tecum

QUINQUAGESIMA: SANCTIFICATION

V. Elegit vos Deus in salutem:
R. In sanctificatione spiritus. 2 *Thess.* 2.13.

Omnipotens sempiterne Deus, cujus Sanctus Spiritus jugiter infusus fidelium corda sanctificat:

Praesta ut ejusdem donis multiplicibus in tuam servitutem utamur, ut vera sapientia docti, intellectu prudentes, firmitate constantes fiamus, et vera scientia instituti et in omni virtute bene fundati te veneremur semper et diligamus: adjuva nos ut muneribus praediti tantis cum populo tuo laetemur quoniam ita sumus creati, redempti, sanctificati; ut in terra sicut

and sanctification, and cheerfully passing our time here on earth as thy loving children, finally with joy to attain eternal life in thy heavenly kingdom; through

ASH WEDNESDAY

V. Cast me not away from thy presence:
R. And take not thy holy Spirit from me. *Ps.* 51.11.

O God our heavenly Father, whose blessed Son was led by the Holy Spirit into the wilderness, there to fast for forty days and forty nights before he was beset by the temptations of evil:

Bless us with the encouragements of the same Spirit as we enter upon this season in faith and repentance: mercifully give us grace to keep the Lenten fast with such devotion that we may bring our emotions and appetites under the control of thy discipline; through

LENT I

V. O give me the comfort of thy help again:
R. And stablish me with thy free Spirit. *Ps.* 51.12.

Almighty and everlasting God, who for the well-being of our earthly life hast put into our hearts wholesome desires of body and spirit:

Mercifully increase and establish in us, we beseech thee, the grace of holy discipline and healthy self-

liberos tibi pios feliciter nos praebeamus, et in regno tuo caelesti tandem aeterna vita fruamur; per

ASH WEDNESDAY

V. Ne projicias me a facie tua:
R. Et Spiritum Sanctum ne auferas a me.

Ps. 50.13.

Deus noster, Pater caelestis, cujus Filius benedictus a Spiritu Sancto in desertum est ductus, ut quadraginta diebus et quadraginta noctibus jejunaret prius quam a diabolo tentaretur:

Adjuva nos, quaesumus, ejusdem Spiritus hortatione, in hoc tempus cum fide et poenitentia ingredientes; concede propitius ut Quadragesimae jejunium ita fideliter observemus, ut affectus nostros et desideria tuae voluntati subjiciamus; per

LENT I

V. Redde mihi laetitiam salutaris tui:
R. Et Spiritu principali confirma me.   *Ps.* 50.14.

Omnipotens sempiterne Deus, qui ut nobis hic viventibus prosint salutaria et corporis et mentis desideria nostris pectoribus inseris:

Clementer, quaesumus, in nobis temperantiam

control; that we may fulfil our desires by the means which thou hast appointed, and for the ends thou ordainest; through

LENT II

V. Make me a clean heart, O God:
R. And renew a right spirit within me. *Ps.* 51.10.

O God, almighty Father, who hast so made us in thine own image that in true freedom we obey thy commandments:

Grant that we may both faithfully employ the strength which is accorded to the spirit of man by thy fatherly ordinance, and also enter upon the inexhaustible riches of thy divine grace and assistance, so that we may obey thee if only we love thee; through

LENT III

V. Thou requirest truth in the inward parts:
R. And shalt make me to understand wisdom secretly.
Ps. 51.6.

O Eternal God, who through thy Son our Lord hast promised a blessing upon those who hear thy Word and faithfully keep it:

Open our ears, we humbly beseech thee, to hear what thou sayest, and enlighten our minds, that what we hear we may understand, and understanding may

sanctam sanamque continentiam confirma et semper adauge, ut quo modo mandavisti et ad id quod praecipis faciendum nostra desideria expleamus; per

LENT II

V. Cor mundum crea in me, Deus:
R. Et spiritum rectum innova in visceribus meis.
Ps. 50.12.

Deus, Pater omnipotens, qui ita nos ad tuam imaginem creavisti, ut in vera libertate tuis mandatis obediamus:

Praesta ut fideliter eas facultates exerceamus quas tu paterna dispositione mentibus hominum es largitus; et infinitis gratiae tuae et auxilii divitiis munerati, obediamus tibi dummodo te diligamus; per

LENT III

V. Veritatem dilexisti:
R. Incerta et occulta sapientiae tuae manifestasti mihi. *Ps.* 50.8.

Sempiterne Deus, qui per Filium tuum, Dominum nostrum, eos beatos esse dixisti qui verbum tuum audiunt et constanter custodiunt: Aperi, quaesumus, aures nostras ut verba tua exaudiamus; mentes

carry into good effect by thy bounteous prompting; through

LENT IV

V. An offering of a free heart will I give thee:
R. And praise thy name, O Lord.   *Ps.* 54.6.

Almighty and everlasting God, with whom in the new Jerusalem above is our freedom:
   We humbly beseech thee so to guide and direct the affections of our hearts that we may always desire to do only such things as shall please thee; through

LENT V

V. I will call upon God:
R. And the Lord shall save me.   *Ps.* 55.17.

Almighty God, Judge of all mankind, whose blessed Son went up to Jerusalem with his disciples, there to accomplish the salvation of the world through his passion:
   Mercifully grant that being redeemed from sin by his precious death upon the Cross, we may be also made partakers of eternal life through his glorious resurrection; who with thee

illumina ut audita intellegamus, intellecta secundum inspirationem tuam bene efficiamus; per

LENT IV

V. Voluntarie sacrificabo tibi, Domine:
R. Et confitebor nomini tuo. *Ps.* 53.8.

Omnipotens sempiterne Deus, quocum in nova Jerusalem in caelis vera libertate fruemur:

Obsecramus te ut affectus nostros ita gubernes, ut semper ea sola facere quae tibi sunt placita cupiamus; per

LENT V

V. Ego ad Deum clamavi:
R. Et Dominus salvabit me. *Ps.* 54.17.

Omnipotens Deus, omnium hominum Judex, cujus Filius benedictus in Jerusalem cum discipulis suis ascendit, ut mundum per passionem suam salvaret:

Concede propitius ut nos, per ejus pretiosam mortem a peccato redempti, per gloriosam ejus resurrectionem aeternae participes vitae fiamus; qui tecum

LENT VI

V. Thou shalt open my lips, O Lord:
R. And my mouth shall show thy praise. *Ps.* 51.15.

O Lord God, heavenly Father, whose blessed Son was received at the gate of Jerusalem with joyful greeting and welcome:

Grant us, we humbly beseech thee, such a measure of abounding love and devout adoration that we may faithfully follow him as our dear Lord and Master, until at the last we attain to the full vision of thy glorious majesty: through

MAUNDY THURSDAY

I. THE FEET-WASHING

V. He made himself of no reputation:
R. And took upon him the form of a servant.
Phil. 2.7.

Almighty and everlasting God, whose blessed Son on the night of his betrayal washed the feet of his Apostles to cleanse them and to teach them humility:

Cleanse us, we beseech thee, from all self-importance and arrogance; and graciously give us such a measure of humility in heart and mind that we may in deed follow him in diligently and dutifully serving the needs of thy people; through

LENT VI

V. Domine, labia mea aperies:
R. Et os meum annuntiabit laudem tuam. *Ps.* 50.17.

Domine Deus, Pater caelestis, cujus Filium benedictum ad portas Jerusalem populus salutationibus laetis accepit:

Obsecramus te ut tantam nobis amoris abundantiam et venerationis piae concedas, ut fideliter eum Dominum carum et Ducem sequamur, donec gloriosam tandem majestatem tuam perfecte intueamur; per

MAUNDY THURSDAY

1. THE FEET-WASHING

V. Semetipsum exinanivit:
R. Formam servi accipiens. *Phil.* 2.7.

Omnipotens sempiterne Deus, cujus Filius benedictus, in nocte qua tradebatur, pedes apostolorum lavit suorum, ut eos mundaret et praeciperet eis humilitatem:

Emunda nos, quaesumus, ab omni superbia et aliorum contemptione; et concede nobis propitius talem cordis et mentis humilitatem, ut pie et diligenter tuis famulis ministrando re vera ejus imitemur exemplum; per

2. THE NEW COMMANDMENT

V. A new commandment I give unto you:
R. That ye love one another. *John* 13.34.

Almighty and everlasting God, whose Son, our Saviour, gave to his apostles in the upper room in Jerusalem the new commandment by which their dealings with others should always be governed and guided:

Mercifully grant, we beseech thee, that we also may loyally accept this sovereign commandment, and joyfully acknowledge his bidding to love one another as the royal rule of our conduct: through

3. THE INSTITUTION OF THE EUCHARIST

V. As often as ye eat this bread and drink this cup:
R. Ye do shew the Lord's death till he come.
  1 *Cor.* 11.26.

Almighty and everlasting God, whose Son, our Saviour Jesus Christ, instituted the holy Sacrament to be a remembrance of his death and passion, and a means whereby we become partakers of his most blessed Body and Blood:

We thank thee with all our hearts for this great gift which is both a precious memorial of his love and a means of grace for mankind until he come again in great glory; and we pray that as true members of his mystical Body we may continually use it with faithful praise and glad thanksgiving; through

2. THE NEW COMMANDMENT

V. Mandatum novum do vobis:
R. Ut diligatis invicem. *Joan.* 13.34.

Omnipotens sempiterne Deus, cujus Filius, Salvator noster, apostolis suis in cenaculo in Jerusalem novum dedit mandatum, quo semper in communicando aliis gubernari deberent:

Clementer, quaesumus, concede ut nos etiam regiae huic legi fideliter obsequamur, et invicem diligendo Domini propositum libenter accipiamus; per

3. THE INSTITUTION OF THE EUCHARIST

V. Quotienscumque manducabitis panem hunc, et calicem bibetis:
R. Mortem Domini annuntiabitis donec veniat.
1 *Cor.* 11.26.

Omnipotens sempiterne Deus, cujus Filius, Salvator noster, Jesus Christus, sanctum instituit sacramentum, per quod mortis ejus et passionis memoriam teneamus, et beatissimi corporis et sanguinis ejus fiamus participes:

Toto tibi cordis affectu gratias agimus, quia nobis pretiosum hoc amoris ejus monumentum donasti, et instrumentum gratiae tuae donec ad nos magna cum gloria redeat; et quoniam vera membra sumus corpori ejus mystico incorporata, oramus ut semper eo fideliter et libenter utamur; per

GOOD FRIDAY

1. A SUFFICIENT SACRIFICE

V. This man after he had offered one sacrifice for sins for ever:

R. Sat down on the right hand of God. *Heb.* 10.12.

Almighty and everlasting God, whose blessed Son, our Saviour Jesus Christ, by his precious death upon the Cross offered thee the one sacrifice which was sufficient to atone for the sins of the whole world:

Mercifully give us grace always to remember this his infinite love which is effectual to salvation for us sinners and for all mankind; and as he sees in us, undeserving as we are, that which draws his love to us, so may we, contrite and humble in heart, offer ourselves through him to thee in fulness of thankful devotion; through

2. A PERFECT OBLATION

V. By this will we are sanctified:

R. Through the offering of the body of Jesus Christ once for all. *Heb.* 10.10.

O eternal Father, whose dear Son Jesus Christ made upon the Cross the oblation of himself which thou dost accept as the perfect offering of reconciliation:

Look with mercy upon us sinners, who by his death are won to be thy sons, and give us grace to receive the

GOOD FRIDAY

1. A SUFFICIENT SACRIFICE

V. Hic autem unam pro peccatis offerens hostiam in sempiternum:
R. Sedet in dextera Dei. *Heb.* 10.12.

Omnipotens sempiterne Deus, cujus Filius benedictus, Salvator noster, Jesus Christus, morte pretiosa unicam tibi in cruce hostiam obtulit, quae expiare peccata totius mundi suffecit:

Da nobis propitius gratiam tuam, ne unquam infiniti ejus amoris obliviscamur, qui nos peccatores et omnes homines valet salvare; et sicut nos quamvis indignos dignatur diligere, ita cum omni gratiarum actione et pietate tibi per illum corda nostra humilia et contrita hostias offeramus; per

2. A PERFECT OBLATION

V. In hac voluntate sanctificati sumus:
R. Per oblationem corporis Jesu Christi semel.
Heb. 10.10.

Pater sempiterne, cujus Filius carus Jesus Christus in cruce sui ipsius fecit oblationem quam tu perfectum accipis piamentum:

Indulgentiam, quaesumus, da peccatoribus nobis qui per ejus mortem filii tui censemur; et gratiam,

full benefit of his great love in true repentance for our sins and certain faith in the power of his sacrifice; through

3. A FULL SATISFACTION

V. We joy in God through our Lord Jesus Christ:
R. By whom we have now received the atonement.

Rom. 5.11.

O heavenly Father, by whose will thy blessed Son our Saviour offered thee satisfaction in full for the sins of all mankind:

Assist us, we beseech thee, humbly to rejoice in the redemption which he wrought for us sinners, who are unable by ourselves to avail ourselves of thy forgiveness; and grant that by the power of his Cross and Passion we may share his victory over sin, and live with him in the eternal joy of thy kingdom; through

EASTER EVEN

V. Christ also hath once suffered for sins:
R. Being put to death in the flesh, but quickened by the Spirit. 1. *Pet.* 3.18.

O Lord, holy Father, whose will it was that the body of thy dear Son after his crucifixion should lie in the tomb while he proclaimed the Gospel of salvation to the spirits of the departed in Paradise:

ut poenitentiam veram agentes, et virtuti oblationis ejus certo animo confidentes, plenum tanti amoris beneficium accipiamus; per

3. A FULL SATISFACTION

V. Gloriamur in Deo per Dominum nostrum Jesum Christum:
R. Per quem nunc reconciliationem accepimus.

Rom. 5.11.

Pater caelestis, cujus voluntate Filius tuus benedictus Salvator noster tibi pro totius mundi peccatis satisfactionem obtulit plenam:

Adjuva nos, quaesumus, ut redemptione quam effecit pro nobis peccatoribus gaudeamus, qui nisi per eum non remissionem tuam adsequi possumus; concede ut per crucis ejus et passionis virtutem cum eo peccatum vincamus, et regni tui gaudio in saecula perfruamur; per

EASTER EVEN

V. Christus semel pro peccatis nostris mortuus est:
R. Mortificatus quidem carne, vivificatus autem spiritu. 1. *Pet.* 3.18.

Domine, sancte Pater, cujus voluntate corpus tui Filii crucifixum in sepulcro jacebat, dum mortuorum spiritibus in Paradiso evangelium praedicabat salutis:

Give us grace, we humbly beseech thee, to believe in his precious death and burial, and to banish and drive away all our fear of the end of this life, in the blessed hope of sharing henceforward in the eternal life he has won for us; through the same

EASTER DAY

V. Thanks be to God, who giveth us the victory:
R. Through our Lord Jesus Christ.   1. *Cor.* 15.57.

O God, whose purpose of saving mankind from sin and death was accomplished in the fulness of time by the rising to life again of thy Son our Saviour Jesus Christ:

Mercifully grant that knowing whence cometh our salvation we may be eager to embrace the benefits thereof, and live in humble hope of resurrection to life everlasting; through the same

EASTER I

V. I am the resurrection and the life:
R. He that believeth in me, though he were dead, yet shall he live.   *John* 11. 25.

O Almighty and everlasting God, who for our salvation didst raise thy Son Jesus Christ from death to life on the third day:

Grant that by faith in his resurrection we may believe beyond a doubt that the source of all life is in

Gratiam, quaesumus, nobis concede ut in pretiosam mortem et sepulturam ejus ita credamus, ut non ex hac vita cedere timeamus, quia spem habemus beatam aeternae vitae ab eo partae dehinc esse consortes; per eundem

EASTER DAY

V. Deo gratias qui dedit nobis victoriam:
R. Per Dominum nostrum Jesum Christum.

1. Cor. 15.57.

Domine Deus, cujus propositum, ut homines a peccatis et a morte salvares, Filii tui Salvatoris nostri resurrectio consummavit, ubi venit temporis plenitudo:

Concede propitius ut nos, scientes unde nostra salus adveniat, ita beneficia ejus studeamus amplecti, ut spem resurgendi ad vitam aeternnam semper humiliter foveamus; per eundem

EASTER I

V. Ego sum resurrectio et vita:
R. Qui credit in me, etiam si mortuus fuerit, vivet.

Joan. 11.25.

Omnipotens sempiterne Deus, qui propter nostram salutem die tertio Filium tuum Jesum Christum a morte ad vitam suscitavisti:

Praesta, quaesumus, ut nos, resurrectionis ejus

thee alone, and that the eternal meaning of our existence can be found only by the light of thy tender love for us; through the same

EASTER II

V. My sheep hear my voice:
R. And I know them, and they follow me.

John 10.27.

O Lord God, whose risen Son proclaimed himself the shepherd of our souls:

Grant, we humbly beseech thee, that we may vigilantly listen for his voice, and hearing it joyfully follow him, so that when he cometh to make a reckoning of those that are his we may be counted among the sheep of his pasture; through the same

EASTER III

V. As often as ye eat this bread and drink this cup:
R. Ye do shew the Lord's death till he come.

1 *Cor.* 11.26.

O God, the resurrection of whose blessed Son hallowed the first day of the week for his disciples:

Give us grace, we humbly beseech thee, truly to commemorate his victory over death by keeping Sunday as a holy day of Christian worship and gladness; through the same

fidem habentes, vitam omnem ex te solo gigni, et per affectum tuum solum posse intelligi pro certo habeamus; per eundem

EASTER II

V. Oves meae vocem meam audiunt:
R. Et ego cognosco eas, et sequuntur me. *Joan.* 10.27.

Domine Deus, cujus Filius, postquam resurrexit a morte, animarum nostrarum pastorem se praedicavit:

Supplices te rogamus ut nos, intente vocem pastoris exaudientes, cum gaudio eum sequamur, ut cum redierit et gregem recensuerit suum, nos quoque inter oves ejus pascuae numeremur; per eundem

EASTER III

V. Quotienscumque manducabitis panem hunc et calicem bibetis:
R. Mortem Domini annuntiabitis donec veniat.

1 *Cor.* 11.26.

Domine Deus, cujus Filius benedictus, resurgendo a morte, primum sabbati discipulis suis sanctificavit:

Supplices te rogamus ut per gratiam tuam resurrectionem ejus vere commemoremus, et diem Dominicam semper adoratione et gaudio consecremus; per eundem

EASTER IV

V. Of his own will begat he us with the word of truth:
R. That we should be a kind of firstfruits of his creatures. *Jas.* 1.18.

O Almighty and everlasting God, who hast decreed that man should be the firstfruits of all thy creation:

Mercifully grant that as thou hast set us at the head of thy creatures, we may be enabled gladly to accept the heavenly gifts of the risen Christ, and diligently to use them in fulfilling his precepts; through the same

EASTER V

V. Make me to go in the path of thy commandments:
R. For therein is my desire. *Ps.* 119.35.

O Lord God, who hast ordered and ordained the life of thy heavenly kingdom in accordance with thy will and intention:

Give us grace, we humbly beseech thee, to rejoice in being thy servants, and gladly to bring all our thoughts and ways into conformity with the laws and commandments of thy fatherly governance; through

EASTER IV

V. Voluntarie genuit nos verbo veritatis:
R. Ut simus initium aliquod creaturae ejus.

Jac. 1.18.

Omnipotens sempiterne Deus, qui homines creaturae tuae esse primitias ordinavisti:

Clementer, quaesumus, concede ut quoniam nos omnium quae creavisti caput esse constituisti, beneficia caelestia Jesu Christi accipere, et in praeceptis ejus implendis diligenter adhibere possimus; per eundem

EASTER V

V. Deduc me in semitam mandatorum tuorum:
R. Quia ipsam volui. *Ps.* 118.35.

Domine Deus, qui regni tui caelestis vitam secundum voluntatem tuam et propositum constituisti:

Supplices te rogamus ut per gratiam tuam quod sumus tui famuli gaudeamus, et quaecumque cogitamus et facimus, omnia legibus et mandatis gubernationis tuae paternae laeti subjiciamus; per

ASCENSION DAY

V. Thou hast ascended on high:
R. Thou hast led captivity captive.   *Ps.* 68.18.

O Almighty and everlasting God, whose blessed Son, after he had accomplished the redemption of mankind from sin and death, ascended to heaven:

Grant that we may continually manifest our thankfulness for the love with which thou didst send him to save us, and endeavour to extend the benefits of the incarnation to all men; through the same

SUNDAY AFTER ASCENSION DAY

V. He hath an unchangeable priesthood:
R. Seeing he ever liveth to make intercession for us.
Heb. 7.24-5.

O Lord God, whose blessed Son is ever pleading before thee the atonement which he made upon the Cross for the sins of the whole world:

Give us grace, unworthy though we be, humbly to join in his heavenly intercession, and to work for the time when all mankind shall joyfully turn to thee in faith and repentance; through the same

ASCENSION DAY

V. Ascendisti in altum:
R. Cepisti captivitatem.   *Ps.* 67.19.

Omnipotens sempiterne Deus, cujus Filius benedictus, postquam homines a morte et peccato redemit, ad caelos ascendit:

Praesta ut nos semper gratias pro affectu tuo agamus, quo eum in salutem nostram misisti, et omnes homines, quoad possimus, beneficiorum incarnationis ejus participes faciamus; per eundem

SUNDAY AFTER ASCENSION DAY

V. Hic autem sempiternum habet sacerdotium:
R. Semper vivens ad interpellandum pro nobis.
Heb. 7.24-5.

Domine Deus, cujus Filius benedictus tibi semper illam repraesentat conciliationem, quam in cruce pro totius mundi peccatis effecit:

Praesta nobis, quamvis indignis, gratiam ut ei sic interpellanti humiliter adjungamur, et laboremus constanter dum omnes homines ad te cum fide et poenitentia convertantur; per eundem

WHITSUN EVE

V. I will pray the Father, and he shall give you another Comforter:

R. That he may abide with you for ever. *John* 14.16.

O Lord God, who through the Ascension of thy blessed Son hast opened again to all men the way to life everlasting:

Give us grace, we humbly beseech thee, so surely to believe in thy perfect love and wisdom, that we may receive with great gladness the power of the Holy Spirit which he has promised to send us; through the same

WHITSUNDAY

V. As many as are led by the Spirit of God:
R. They are the sons of God. *Rom.* 8.14.

O Almighty everlasting God, who on the day of Pentecost didst send thy Holy Spirit with power to join together in the work of the Church all those who believe in thee:

Mercifully grant that by the operation of the same gracious Spirit all Christian people, united in thee and with thee in the Church of Christ Jesus, may remain steadfast in its teaching and fellowship and delight in its worship, until after this life we may be admitted to the full joy of perfect discipleship; through the same

WHITSUN EVE

V. Ego rogabo Patrem, et alium Paracletum dabit vobis:

R. Ut maneat vobiscum in aeternum. *Joan.* 14.16.

Domine Deus, qui per Filii tui benedicti Ascensionem aeternae vitae viam omnibus hominibus rursus aperuisti:

Humiliter te obsecramus ut nos, affectui tuo et sapientiae confidentes, Sancti Spiritus virtutem laeti accipiamus, quam se nobis esse missurum promisit; per eundem

WHITSUNDAY

V. Quicumque Spiritu Dei aguntur:
R. Ii sunt filii Dei. *Rom.* 8.14.

Omnipotens sempiterne Deus, qui die Pentecostes Spiritum tuum Sanctum misisti, ut potestate sua omnes qui in te credunt ad opus Ecclesiae perficiendum conjungeret:

Clementer praesta ut per ejusdem Spiritus virtutem Christiani omnes, in Ecclesia Jesu Christi tecum conjuncti, in doctrina ejus et societate perseverantes, et in adoratione ejus gaudentes, tandem post hanc vitam ad plena obsequii tui gaudia veniamus; per eundem

TRINITY SUNDAY

V. Holy, holy, holy:
R. Lord God Almighty. *Rev.* 4.8.

O God, who hast made thyself known to us as Trinity in Unity and Unity in Trinity, in order that we may be informed of thy love and thy majesty:

Mercifully grant that we may not be terrified by what thou hast revealed of thy majesty, nor tempted to trespass upon thy mercy by what we know of thy love for us; but that by the power of thy Spirit we may be for ever drawn to thee in true adoration and worship; who livest and reignest, one God, world without end.

TRINITY I

V. Beloved, if God so loved us;
R. We ought also to love one another. 1 *John* 4.11.

O God, our Creator and Guide, who hast given to us thy creatures the desire to obey thee:

Enable us to love thee as thou hast loved us, by giving ourselves to thy service in praise and thanksgiving all the days of our lives; through

TRINITY SUNDAY

V. Sanctus, sanctus, sanctus:
R. Domine Deus Omnipotens. *Apoc.* 4.8.

Domine Deus, qui teipsum Trinitatem in Unitate et Unitatem in Trinitate esse nos docuisti, ut de affectu tuo et majestate certiores fiamus:

Concede propitius ne propter quodcumque tuae majestatis revelasti deterreamur, neve, quodcumque affectus tui cognovimus, tuam clementiam praesumamus, sed ut per Spiritus tui virtutem ad te semper in vera adoratione ducamur; qui vivis et regnas Deus per omnia saecula saeculorum.

TRINITY I

V. Carissimi, si sic Deus dilexit nos.
R. Et nos debemus alterutrum diligere.

1 *Joan.* 4.11.

Domine Deus, noster dux et creator, qui nobis creaturis tuis desiderium tibi obsequendi dedisti:

Praesta ut quomodo tu nos dilexisti, ita teipsum diligamus, et in laude tua et gratiarum actione per omnes vitae dies servitio nos tuo devoveamus; per

TRINITY II

V. God is love:

R. And he that dwelleth in love, dwelleth in God, and God in him. 1 *John* 4.16.

O God, the Father almighty, who of thy great love towards mankind didst give thine only-begotten Son to be the propitiation for our sins:

Grant that we may daily grow in knowledge of thee and love thee more, and each other for thy sake; through

TRINITY III

V. This commandment have we from him:

R. That he who loveth God, love his brother also.
1 John 4.21.

O God, who art the Father of the whole family of mankind:

Implant in us such brotherly love and affection that we may never be prevented from relieving the needs and distress of our neighbours by enmity and prejudice or by the blindness of our own concerns; and give us the will always to succour others but never to spare ourselves in the service of thy Son our Lord Jesus Christ; who liveth

TRINITY II

V. Deus caritas est:
R. Et qui manet in caritate, in Deo manet, et Deus
   in eo.   I *Joan*. 4.16.

Deus, Pater omnipotens, qui pro tua humani generis caritate Filium unigenitum tuum dedisti, ut pro peccatis nostris esset propitiatio:

Concede ut nos in scientia tui quotidie augeamur, et teipsum magis in dies et tui causa alterutrum amemus; per

TRINITY III

V. Hoc mandatum habemus a Deo:
R. Ut qui diligit Deum, diligat et fratrem suum.
                                         I *Joan*. 4.21.

Deus, qui humanae totius es Pater familiae:

Insere, quaesumus, nostris cordibus tantum fraterni amoris affectum, ut nunquam, invidia vel iniquitate vel hujus saeculi cura caecati, aliorum necessitatibus subvenire nolimus; et voluntatem concede, ut semper alios adjuvare, nobis ipsis nunquam parcere studeamus, in servitio Filii tui Jesu Christi; Qui tecum

TRINITY IV

V. Be ye followers of God, as dear children:
R. And walk in love, as Christ also hath loved us.
Eph. 5.1-2.

O Lord Jesus Christ, who didst both command thine apostles that they should love one another, and give thyself to suffer for their sakes:

Grant that we may, in what we do and in what we give, follow thine example of service and sacrifice, that we may ever be faithful and obedient in our Christian vocation; who livest

TRINITY V

V. There is no fear in love:
R. But perfect love casteth out fear.   1 *John* 4.18.

O Lord God, who though not seen by any man at any time, hast yet revealed thyself to all who believe in thee:

Grant us that perfectness of love which banishes all fear, and vouchsafe that we may stand with boldness before thee at the day of judgment, having proved ourselves obedient to the precept of thy Son, Jesus Christ; who liveth

TRINITY IV

V. Estote imitatores Dei, sicut filii carissimi:
R. Et ambulate in dilectione, sicut et Christus
   dilexit nos. *Eph.* 5.1-2.

Domine Jesu Christe, qui apostolis tuis praeceptum mandasti ut diligerent invicem, et teipsum dedisti ut pro eis tormentum subires:

Concede ut quaecumque faciamus et quaecumque demus, obsequii et oblationis tuum imitemur exemplum, et officium vocatione dignum et fidelitatem tibi semper praestemus; qui vivis

TRINITY V

V. Timor non est in caritate:
R. Sed perfecta caritas foras mittit timorem.
   1 *Joan.* 4.18.

Domine Deus, quem nemo unquam adspexit, qui tamen te omnibus qui in te credunt manifestum fecisti:

Da nobis perfectam eam caritatem quae foras mittit timorem, et praesta ut coram te in die judicii fiduciam habeamus, quoniam praecepta Filii tui Jesus Christi erimus obsecuti; qui tecum

TRINITY VI

V. Blessed is he whose unrighteousness is forgiven, and whose sin is covered:
R. Blessed is the man unto whom the Lord imputeth no sin. *Ps.* 32.1.

Cleanse, we beseech thee, O Lord, our hearts and minds with the most merciful fountain of thy grace, that we may ever abide by thy commandments in spirit and in truth; and so enlighten our consciences as thou dost enrich our minds, that our love for thee and our neighbours for thy sake may suppress in us all covetousness, pride, and malice, and keep a constant guard on our words and thoughts as well as on our deeds; through

TRINITY VII

V. Now being made free from sin, and become servants of God:
R. Ye have your fruit unto holiness, and the end everlasting life. *Rom.* 6.22.

Almighty God, Maker of all things, Judge of all men, who at the last day wilt separate man from man as sheep from goats according to their lives:

Keep, we beseech thee, our bodies and our souls servants of righteousness, that we may yield fruit unto holiness, and in the end attain unto everlasting life; through

TRINITY VI

V. Beati quorum remissae sunt iniquitates, et quorum tecta sunt peccata:
R. Beatus vir cui non imputavit Dominus peccatum.
Ps. 31.1.

Corda, quaesumus, Domine, nostra et mentes emunda gratiae tuae fonte et misericordiae, ut nos in spiritu et in veritate semper tuis mandatis adhaereamus: et quomodo mentes locupletasti, ita conscientias nostras illumina, ut teipsum et proximos tui causa, diligendo avaritiam omnem et malitiam et superbiam superemus, et cogitationes verba opera nostra jugiter custodiamus; per

TRINITY VII

V. Nunc vero liberati a peccato, servi autem facti Deo, habetis fructum vestrum in sanctificationem:
R. Finem vero vitam aeternam. *Rom.* 6.22.

Deus omnipotens, rerum omnium Creator, hominum omnium Judex, qui in extremo die sicut oves ab haedis homines ab invicem secundum ipsorum opera separabis:

Fac, quaesumus, ut corpora nostra et animae ita justitiae famulentur, ut fructum ipsi in sanctificationem feramus, donec ad vitam aeternam perveniamus; per

TRINITY VIII

V. Ye have not received the spirit of bondage again to fear:
R. But ye have received the spirit of adoption, whereby we cry, Abba, Father. *Rom.* 8.15.

Almighty and merciful Father, who willest not that thy creatures should perish through their own inventions, but rather that they should live as thy sons by adoption and grace:

Grant that we may show ourselves to be called joint-heirs with Christ, by so suffering with him that we may enter into his glory; who liveth

TRINITY IX

V. My son, if thou comest to serve the Lord, prepare thy soul for temptation.
R. Set thy heart aright, and constantly endure.
Ecclus. 2.1.

O merciful Lord, whose blessed Son endured temptation to the uttermost, and was obedient to thy will unto death for the redemption of mankind:

Grant that our frail wills may be so strengthened by thy grace that the temptations that beset us may not overmaster us, but rather become the means of our probation in thy sight; through the same

TRINITY VIII

V. Non accepistis spiritum servitutis iterum in timore:

R. Sed accepisitis spiritum adoptionis filiorum, in quo clamamus: Abba (Pater). *Rom.* 8.15.

Pater omnipotens et misericors, qui non vis eos quos creavisti suis ipsorum adinventionibus interire, sed sicut filios tuos per adoptionem et gratiam vivere:

Praesta ut nos ipsi vere Christi coheredes videamur vocari, cum passionis ejus fiamus participes ut in gloriam ejus intremus; qui tecum

TRINITY IX

V. Fili, accedens ad servitutem Dei, praepara animam tuam ad temptationem:

R. Deprime cor tuum, et sustine. *Ecclus.* 2.1.

Domine misericors, cujus Filius benedictus tentationem sustinebat extremam, voluntati tuae usque ad mortem factus obediens, ut homines omnes redimerentur:

Concede ut voluntatum nostrarum infirmitas ita tua gratia confortetur, ut non eis quae nos circumdant tentationibus superemur, sed ut per eas in tuo conspectu probemur; per eundem

TRINITY X

V. There are diversities of gifts, but the same Spirit:
R. And there are diversities of operations, but it is the same God, which worketh all in all.

1 Cor. 12.4,6

Almighty and everlasting God, who hast revealed thyself in all thy power through the incarnation of thy Son, Jesus Christ our Lord, and who dwellest in us by the working of thy Holy Spirit:

Grant that we may, each in his several calling, profit from the operation of that one and the self-same Spirit whose gifts are manifold, to the glory of thy holy name, Father, Son, and Holy Ghost, world without end.

TRINITY XI

V. Everyone that exalteth himself shall be abased:
R. And he that humbleth himself shall be exalted.

Luke 18.14.

Almighty God, only giver of all mercies, whose Son, Jesus Christ, has taught us how to pray aright:

Save us, we beseech thee, from all presumptuousness in our prayer, and grant unto us the grace of humility and contrition; that we may, sharing the vision of thine Apostle Saint Paul, know that it is by thy grace alone that we are what we are, and that we can do nothing but through the strengthening of thy Son, Christ our Lord; who liveth

TRINITY X

V. Divisiones vero gratiarum sunt, idem autem Spiritus:
R. Et divisiones operationum sunt, idem vero Deus, qui operatur omnia in omnibus. 1 *Cor.* 12.4,6.

Omnipotens sempiterne Deus, qui teipsum in omni virtute tua revelavisti per incarnationem Filii tui Jesu Christi, Domini nostri, et per operationem Sancti tui Spiritus in nobis inhabitas:

Praesta ut nos omnes, in sua quisque vocatione, ex operatione ejusdem unius Spiritus, cujus multiformes sunt gratiae, fructum percipiamus, ad gloriam nominis tui sancti, Patris, Filii, et Sancti Spiritus in saecula saeculorum.

TRINITY XI

V. Omnis qui se exaltat, humiliabitur:
R. Et qui se humiliat, exaltabitur. *Luc.* 18.14.

Omnipotens Deus, dator omnium misericordiarum, cujus Filius, Jesus Christus, nos recte orationes facere docuit:

Quaesumus ut dum oramus ab omni audacia liberemur, et gratiis humilitatis et poenitentiae impleamur; concede ut nos, sicut Sanctus Paulus, apostolus tuus, agnoscamus nos non nisi gratia tua id esse quod simus, neque quicquam nisi Filii tui Jesu Christi virtute et auxilio posse perficere; qui tecum

TRINITY XII

V. My tongue shall sing of thy word:
R. For all thy commandments are righteous.

Ps. 119.172.

O gracious God, whose blessed Son set forth thy love towards mankind, in his miracles of healing and mercy, making both the deaf to hear and the dumb to speak:

Grant that our ears may be opened to hear thy word, and our tongues loosed to proclaim it to others, and to further the spreading of thy gospel among all nations; through the same

TRINITY XIII

V. Ye have purified your souls unto unfeigned love of the brethren:
R. See that ye love one another with a pure heart fervently. 1 *Pet.* 1.22.

Almighty and all-loving God, whose tender mercy towards mankind is the pattern of our love one to another:

Grant that, loving our fellow men, and caring for them, we may seek and find opportunities for thy service; that so we may turn aside from our own business to the relief of suffering and distress, and fulfil the commandment of our Lord Jesus Christ; who liveth

TRINITY XII

V. Pronuntiabit lingua mea eloquium tuum:
R. Quia omnia mandata tua aequitas.   *Ps.* 118.172.

Deus misericors, cujus Filius benedictus affectum tuum erga humanum genus ita sanitatis et misericordiae signis ostendit ut surdos audire et mutos eloqui faceret:

Praesta ut nos apertis auribus tuum eloquium audiamus et solutis linguis pronuntiemus, quo latius inter gentes omnes tuum evangelium diffundatur; per eundem

TRINITY XIII

V. Animas vestras castificantes in fraternitatis amore:
R. Simplici ex corde invicem diligite attentius.
                                     1 *Pet.* 1.22.

Omnipotens benignissime Deus, qui ita homines dilexisti, ut nobis exemplum praebueris quo invicem diligamus:

Praesta ut nos, fraternitatem hominum curando et diligendo, semper tibi ipsi serviendi occasionem inveniamus, et nostra negotia abnegantes miseris et afflictis subministremus, secundum mandata Domini nostri Jesu Christi; qui tecum

TRINITY XIV

V. Awake thou that sleepest, and arise from the dead:
R. And Christ shall give thee light.   *Eph.* 5.14.

Almighty God, who by the incarnation of thy Son, Jesus Christ, hast consecrated our manhood to thy service, and hast afforded us the means of grace that we should not be bound by the nature of our flesh and the lusts thereof:

So direct our souls and bodies that we may perceive the fruits of thy Holy Spirit, and grant that we may truly love our neighbours as ourselves, living together in long-suffering, joy, and peace, and finally become inheritors of thy kingdom, where thy Son reigneth for evermore, our Lord and Saviour, Jesus Christ.

TRINITY XV

V. Seek ye first the kingdom of God, and his righteousness:
R. And all these things shall be added unto you.
Matt. 6.33.

Cleanse our minds, O Lord, we beseech thee, of all anxious thoughts for ourselves, that we may learn not to trust in the abundance of what we have save as tokens of thy goodness and grace, but that we may commit ourselves in faith to thy keeping, and devote all our energy of soul, mind, and body to the work of

TRINITY XIV

V. Surge, qui dormis, et exsurge a mortuis:
R. Et illuminabit te Christus. *Eph.* 5.14.

Omnipotens Deus, qui per incarnationem Filii tui Jesu Christi nos homines ad tuam servitutem sanctificasti, et nobis gratiae instrumenta donasti, ne carnis nostrae natura et desideriis alligemur:

Ita, quaesumus, animas nostras et corpora dirige, ut Sancti tui Spiritus fructum percipiamus, et praesta ut vere diligentes proximos sicut nos ipsos, cum eis in gaudio, pace, patientia conversemur, et tandem regni tui heredes fiamus, ubi regnat in saecula saeculorum Dominus noster et Salvator Jesus Christus.

TRINITY XV

V. Quaerite primum regnum Dei et justitiam ejus:
R. Et haec omnia adjicientur vobis. *Matt.* 6.33.

Mentes, quaesumus, nostras, Domine Deus, emunda ab omni sollicitudine, ne in possessionibus nostris, nisi ut in caritatis tuae et gratiae signis, confidentiam habeamus, sed ut nos ipsos tibi fidenter in custodiam commendemus; et praesta ut unusquisque nostrum totis animae mentis corporis viribus in regni tui

thy kingdom and the furthering of the purposes of thy divine righteousness; through

TRINITY XVI

V. Strengthen us, O Lord, with might by thy Spirit in the inner man:
R. That Christ may dwell in our hearts by faith.
after Eph. 3.16-17.

Almighty God, who once didst promise thy faithful people through thy prophet that thou wouldest put thy law in their inward parts and write it in their hearts:

Grant to us who know thee through thy Son, Jesus Christ, that we may be filled with that love which transcends law and passes knowledge, and so become lively vessels of the fulness of thy grace; through

TRINITY XVII

V. Whosoever exalteth himself shall be abased:
R. And he that humbleth himself shall be exalted.
Luke 14.11.

Almighty God, who hast given to every man talents to use, and hast ordained for him a vocation for thy service:

Grant us that humility and faithfulness that we may accept the tasks allotted to us in our several callings,

opere faciendo utatur, et divinae tuae justitiae propositis obsequendo; per

TRINITY XVI

V. Corrobora nos, Domine, virtute per Spiritum tuum in interiorem hominem:

R. Ut Christus habitet per fidem in cordibus nostris.
after Eph. 3.16-17.

Deus Omnipotens, qui per prophetam tuum olim fideli tuo populo promisisti, te legem tuam in visceribus eorum daturum et in corde eorum scripturum:

Da nobis, quaesumus, qui te per Filium tuum Jesum Christum cognovimus, ut eo affectu impleamur amoris qui exsuperat legem et super scientiam eminet, et viva tuae gratiae plenitudinis vasa fiamus; per

TRINITY XVII

V. Omnis qui se exaltat, humiliabitur:
R. Et qui se humiliat, exaltabitur. *Luc.* 14.11.

Deus Omnipotens, qui unicuique homini talenta in usum dedisti, et vocationem ei ad tuum servitium praescripsisti:

Da nobis eam fidem et humilitatem, ut omnes in

and that we may esteem ourselves as nothing except in thy service: grant this for the sake of thy Son, Jesus Christ, who himself performed the task that thou didst appoint him to fulfil; who liveth

TRINITY XVIII

V. Thou shalt love the Lord thy God with all thy heart, and with all thy soul, and with all thy mind:
R. And thy neighbour as thyself. *Matt.* 22.37-39.

O Lord Jesus Christ, who by thy coming among us under the veil of the flesh, didst set up a ladder between heaven and earth:

Grant that we may so love our neighbours and brethren whom we can see, that we may love God whom we cannot see save through thee; who livest

TRINITY XIX

V. Be ye kind one to another, tender-hearted, forgiving one another:
R. Even as God for Christ's sake hath forgiven you.
Eph. 4.32.

Almighty God, whose blessed Son Jesus Christ did teach us the lessons of charity and forgiveness:

Grant us by the true conversion of our hearts and minds that we may turn away from that esteem of ourselves which leads to lies and slander, anger and

vocationibus nostris quicquid erit mandatum accipiamus, et nosmetipsos pro nihilo nisi in tuo servitio aestimemus; hoc praesta Filii tui causa Jesu Christi, qui mandatum tuum ipse est adsecutus; qui tecum

TRINITY XVIII

V. Diliges Dominum Deum tuum ex toto corde tuo et in tota anima tua et in tota mente tua:
R. Et proximum tuum sicut teipsum. *Matt.* 22.37-39.

Domine Jesu Christe, qui inter nos homines sub velamine carnis descendere es dignatus, ut quasi scalam inter caelum et terram erigeres:

Praesta ut ita diligamus fratres nostros et proximos quos possumus videre, ut Deum quoque verius diligamus, quem non nisi per te videmus; qui vivis

TRINITY XIX

V. Estote invicem benigni, misericordes, donantes invicem:
R. Sicut et Deus in Christo donavit vobis.

Eph. 4.32.

Deus Omnipotens, cujus Filius benedictus Jesus Christus nos diligere invicem et dimittere docuit:

Praesta ut per veram cordium et mentium con-

bitterness, and that we may attain to a true understanding of others with a grateful heart and a forgiving mind, for the sake of him who forgave his enemies on the Cross; who liveth

TRINITY XX

V. There shall be weeping and gnashing of teeth:
R. For many are called, but few are chosen.
Matt. 22.13-14.

O Lord God, the source of all grace and the judge of all men, who hast invited us to enter thy Kingdom, but dost not force our wills to obedience:

Grant that we may so use thy present grace that we may not have cause to fear thy final judgement; through

TRINITY XXI

V. Put on the whole armour of God:
R. That ye may be able to stand against the wiles of the devil. *Eph.* 6.11.

Almighty God, who dost require of thy soldiers faithful and constant service and discipline:

Enable us to use fearlessly the heavenly armour that thou hast provided for the spiritual warfare; and grant that we may, boldly confronting falsehood and vice with truth and righteousness, always stand

versionem ab ea superbia liberemur, cujus fructus
est mendacium et ira et amaritudo; et ut proximos
grato et misericordi animo vere noscamus, per eum
qui inimicis suis in cruce dimisit; qui tecum

TRINITY XX

V. Ibi erit fletus et stridor dentium:
R. Multi enim sunt vocati, pauci vero electi.

Matt. 22.13-14.

Domine Deus, totius fons gratiae, hominum omnium
judex, qui nos in tuum regnum invitavisti, neque
tamen voluntatem nostram in obsequium cogis:

Praesta ut gratia tua in praesenti ita utamur ut in
novissimo die judicium tuum non timeamus; per

TRINITY XXI

V. Induite vos armaturam Dei:
R. Ut possitis stare adversus insidias diaboli.

Eph. 6.11.

Deus omnipotens, qui a militibus tuis quaeris ut
constanter et fideliter obsequium tibi et officium praestent:

Da, quaesumus, ut armatura caelesti, quam ad
bellum spirituale suppeditas, sine timore uti possimus; et concede ut nos, nequitiae et mendacio veritatem et justitiam fortiter opponentes, et fidei nostrae

firm behind the shield of our faith, and persevere in supplication and vigilance; through

TRINITY XXII

V. Pray that your love may abound yet more and more in knowledge:
R. That ye may approve things that are excellent.

Phil. 1.9.

Lord, to whom belongeth all forgiveness and love:

We beseech thee that we may grow in compassion towards all with whom we have to do, at home and abroad, that we may learn to understand them better in their strength and in their weakness, in their sorrow and in their joy; and grant that by so learning to forgive others we may begin ourselves to deserve forgiveness; through

TRINITY XXIII

V. Our citizenship is in heaven:
R. From whence also we look for the Saviour.

Phil. 3.20.

Almighty God, whose Son Jesus Christ condescended to the citizenship of this world, that we, by his grace, might ascend to the citizenship of heaven:

Grant that we may be so throughly converted from the self-seeking standards of the world that the

scuto protecti, semper in vigilantia et obsecratione perstemus; per

TRINITY XXII

V. Orate ut caritas vestra magis ac magis abundet in scientia:
R. Ut probetis potiora. *Phil.* 1.9.

Domine Deus, cui propria est caritas omnis et remissio peccatorum:

Oramus te ut erga omnes, inter quos et domi et foris versemur, magis ac magis misericordes fiamus, ut eorum virtutem et infirmitatem, tristitiam et gaudium melius intelligamus; et praesta ut nos ita aliis remittere discendo ipsi quoque mereamur aliquando remissionem; per

TRINITY XXIII

V. Nostra conversatio in caelis est:
R. Unde etiam Salvatorem exspectamus.

Phil. 3.20.

Deus Omnipotens, cujus Filius benedictus Jesus Christus hujus mundi civis fieri est dignatus, ut nos per ejus gratiam in civitatem caelestem ascenderemus:

Praesta ut nos ab humana cupiditate ita penitus convertamur, ut corpora humilitatis nostrae corpori

bodies of our low estate may be conformed to his glorious body, as our wills assume the pattern of his will, who made himself obedient even unto death.

TRINITY XXIV

V. Pray that ye might be filled with the knowledge of God's will in all wisdom and spiritual understanding:

R. And that ye might walk worthy of the Lord unto all pleasing. *Col.* 1.9-10.

O bountiful Lord, who hast entrusted us with the stewardship of thy talents:

Grant us such enlightenment of our conscience as may direct our understanding according to thy will; that as we increase in knowledge, so we may daily do thee more worthy service; through

TRINITY XXV

V. Jesus said, He that cometh to me shall never hunger:

R. And he that believeth on me shall never thirst.

John. 6.35.

O Almighty God, whose blessed Son holds in his foreknowledge all the needs of thy people:

Mercifully grant that we may so prepare ourselves

claritatis ejus configurentur, sicut voluntates nostrae voluntatis ejus fiunt conformes, qui obediens factus est usque ad mortem.

TRINITY XXIV

V. Orate ut impleamini agnitione voluntatis ejus in omni scientia et intellectu spiritali:
R. Ut ambuletis digne Deo per omnia placentes.

Col. 1.9-10.

Domine benignissime, qui nos talentorum tuorum dispensatores fecisti:

Illumina, quaesumus, conscientiam nostram ut voluntati tuae intellectum subjiciamus; et praesta ut quo magis in agnitione tui proficiamus, eo dignius tibi in dies obsequamur; per

TRINITY XXV

V. Dixit Jesus, Qui venit ad me, non esuriet:
R. Et qui credit in me, non sitiet unquam.

Joan. 6.35.

Deus omnipotens, cujus Filius benedictus quodcumque opus sit populo tuo praescientia sua complectitur:

for his coming that we may be worthy to be guests at his table and partakers of that bread of God which cometh down from heaven as the sign of grace and the means of life everlasting;

Concede propitius ut nos in ejus adventum parati ad mensam ejus invitemur, et panis Dei illius, qui de caelo descendit ut gratiae signum sit et vitae instrumentum aeternae, digni fiamus participes;

Groups of Prayers

FOR SUNDAYS
IN ADVENT, THE NEW YEAR,
EPIPHANY, LITTLE LENT,
AND TRINITY

THREE PRAYERS FOR ADVENT SUNDAY

I

Let us pray for grace to make a right beginning of the new Church Year.

V. Now it is high time to awake out of sleep:
R. For now is our salvation nearer than when we believed. *Rom.* 13.11.

O Lord God, author of our salvation, who desirest that all men should live in Christ Jesus:

Grant that we may begin this new year in our spiritual life knowing our need to increase our faith and to enlarge our repentance; assist us in thy mercy to live as in a state of grace, and to regard this life as part of our eternal inheritance; grant that difficulties may not overthrow us nor temptations defeat us, but that we may go forward on our journey through this life in the spirit of courage and godliness; through the same

THREE PRAYERS FOR ADVENT SUNDAY

I

Gratiam rogemus ut annum novum Sanctae Ecclesiae recte incipiamus.

V. Hora est jam nos de somno surgere:
R. Nunc enim propior est nostra salus quam cum credidimus. *Rom.* 13.11.

Domine Deus, salutis nostrae auctor, qui homines in Christo Jesu vivere voluisti:

Concede ut nos, vitae spiritualis annum hunc novum incipientes, sciamus opus esse fidem nostram et poenitentiam adaugere: et propitius adjuva nos ut in salutari viventes hanc vitam patrimonii nostri sempiterni partem esse intelligamus; et inter difficultates et tentationes invicti per hanc vitam pie et fortiter progrediamur; per eundem

2

Let us pray that we may be ready for Christ's Second coming.

V. As the Father raiseth up the dead, and quickeneth them:
R. Even so the Son quickeneth whom he will.

John 5.21.

O Lord, Holy Father, who hast committed all judgment to thy Son our Saviour Christ Jesus:

We humbly beseech thee graciously to direct our hearts in such good courses that we may be ready at his second coming to greet him with joyfulness; through the same

3

Let us pray for an increase in Christian wisdom.

V. As ye received of us how ye ought to walk, and to please God:
R. So ye would abound more and more.

1 *Thess.* 4.1.

O Lord God, by the guidance of whose Holy Spirit the Church leads our thoughts along the paths of orderly truthfulness:

We thank thee for the yearly sequence of meditation on the Christian mysteries and of the consecration of our life by the observance of the Saviour's teaching: grant us year by year a firmer understanding

2

Oremus ut Christi reditum paratis animis exspectemus.

V. Sicut Pater suscitat mortuos et vivificat:
R. Sic et Filius quos vult vivificat.   *Joan.* 5.21.

Domine Deus, Pater sanctissime, qui omne judicium Filio tuo Salvatori nostro mandasti:

Humiliter obsecramus ut animas nostras ita recto cursu propitius dirigas, ut eum cum iterum advenerit laeti accipiamus; per eundem

3

Oremus ut sapientia Christiana nobis augeatur.

V. Quemadmodum accepistis a nobis quomodo oporteat vos ambulare et placere Deo:
R. Sic et ambuletis, ut abundetis magis. 1 *Thess.* 4.1.

Domine Deus, cujus Sancto Spiritu ducente Ecclesia tua nos veritatem et disciplinam adsequi docet:

Gratiam tibi agimus quia mysteria tua per annum totum ex ordine meditanda proponit, ut doctrina Salvatoris observanda vitam quotidie tibi dedicare possimus: concede, quaesumus, ut in singulos annos melius veritatem aeternam noscamus, affectum tuum amoris magis percipiamus, inspirationi tuae fidentius innitamur; ut nobis hic in terra peregrinantibus cae-

of eternal truth, a deeper knowledge of thy love, and a more confident reliance on thy holy leadership; that as we pass through the years of our pilgrimage here on earth we may increase in heavenly wisdom until we reach the kingdom in which alone is true freedom; through the same

FOUR PRAYERS FOR ADVENT II

I

Let us pray that the study of the Scriptures may fulfil God's purpose for them in our hearts.

V. The God of hope fill you:
R. With all joy and peace in believing.   *Rom.* 15.13.

O Almighty and everlasting God, who hast graciously made known to us through the Scriptures the love that thou hast for us:

Give us grace, we humbly beseech thee, so to study the Bible and think upon its meaning, that we may thankfully acknowledge the glory which thy revelation makes known to us, and call to our aid thy Holy Spirit that we may partake of thy blessings; through

lestis sapientia crescat, donec ad regnum caelorum, solum verae libertatis domicilium, veniamus; per eundem

FOUR PRAYERS FOR ADVENT II

I

Oremus ut meditando Sacras Scripturas Dei propositum in cordibus impleamus.

V. Deus spei repleat vos:
R. Omni gaudio et pace in credendo.   *Rom.* 15.13.

Omnipotens sempiterne Deus, qui nobis per Sacras Scripturas affectum tuum amoris propitius monstravisti:

Humiliter obsecramus ut earum verba perlegentes ita quae significant percipiamus, ut gloriam quam nobis indicas cognoscamus, et Sancti tui Spiritus auxilio benedictionis tuae fiamus participes; per

2

Let us pray for grace to use the Bible rightly.

V. Whatsoever things were written aforetime:
R. Were written for our learning. *Rom.* 15.4.

O God, who from age to age hast revealed thy will and pleasure through the utterances and writings of holy men:

We humbly thank thee for the gift of the Bible; we thank thee for the courage of the prophets; the zeal of evangelists; the vision of poets; the search for truth by historians; we thank thee for their faithful response to the inspiration of thy good guidance: give us grace to make full use of this precious heritage, and by prayer and meditation on its message continually to advance in our knowledge of thee and thy will for us; through

3

Let us pray that we may understand the teaching of the Old Testament.

V. Jesus Christ was a minister of the circumcision for the truth of God:
R. To confirm the promises made unto the fathers.
Rom. 15.8.

O God, the God of those who have gone before us, who art the same as yesterday to us today and for ever:

2

Gratiam rogemus ut Sacris Scripturis recte utamur.

V. Quaecumque scripta sunt:
R. Ad nostram doctrinam scripta sunt.   *Rom.* 15.4.

Domine Deus, qui per saecula voluntatem tuam dictis et scriptis sanctorum hominum revelasti:

Tibi humiliter gratias agimus quia nobis Sacras Scripturas dedisti: quia fortes tui prophetae, evangelistae studiosi, perspicaces poetae, sectatores veritatis historici, tam fideliter tibi gubernanti sunt obsecuti; concede ut his libris sicut pretiosa hereditate utamur, et orando et verba eorum perlegendo plenius in dies teipsum et voluntatem tuam intelligamus; per

3

Oremus ut Veteris Testamenti doctrinam recte intelligamus.

V. Christus Jesus minister fuit circumcisionis propter veritatem Dei:
R. Ad confirmandas promissiones patrum. *Rom.* 15.8.

Domine Deus, qui eorum Deus es qui nos antecesserunt, qui hodie idem es atque heri et in saecula saeculorum:

Grant that we may profitably ponder on the records of the fathers of old time, and have confidence that the promises of help which thou didst graciously fulfil to them in danger and distress will be fulfilled to us also; that we may know that thou dost not desert those whom thou lovest, and that thy hand is over them for good in their doings, to lead them to safety and peace everlasting; through

4

Let us pray for grace to study the words of our Lord as the revelation of the Father.

V. That ye may with one mind and mouth glorify God:
R. Even the Father of our Lord Jesus Christ.

Rom. 15.6.

O Almighty and everlasting God, who hast graciously shown thyself to us through thy Son, our Saviour Jesus Christ:

Give us grace, we humbly beseech thee, to study his words, to think upon their meaning, and thankfully to acknowledge the eternal glory which they make known to us; through the same

Concede, quaesumus, ut nos acta patrum antiquorum in lucrum nostrum recenseamus, credentes te promissiones quas eis inter pericula et necessitates confirmavisti, nobis quoque auxiliando ita esse confirmaturum, ut videamus te quos diligis eos nunquam deserere, sed manu tua in actis omnibus ad salutem et pacem sempiternam dirigere; per

4

Gratiam rogemus ut Domini nostri verba meditantes Patris revelationem agnoscamus.

V. Ut unanimes uno ore honorificetis Deum:
R. Et Patrem Domini nostri Jesu Christi. *Rom.* 15.6.

Omnipotens sempiterne Deus, qui per Filium tuum Salvatorem nostrum Jesum Christum nobis teipsum propitius revelasti:

Concede nobis, humiliter obsecramus, ut verba ejus recordati significationem eorum meditemur, et aeternam gloriam quae in eis monstratur gratis animis agnoscamus; per eundem

FIVE PRAYERS FOR ADVENT III

I

Let us give thanks to God for the Ministry of the Church.

V. Let a man so account of us:
R. As of the ministers of Christ, and stewards of the mysteries of God.   1 *Cor.* 4.1.

Almighty and everlasting God, whose blessed Son, the unwearying great high priest of all mankind, presents for us before thee intercession unceasing:

We thank thee for the labours of the clergy of thy holy Church from the day of Pentecost until now: for the oversight and ministration of the bishops in their sees; for the pastoral activity of priests and deacons in the mission field and in their parishes; for their guidance in doctrine, for their leading in worship, for their recollection in prayer and for their perseverance in the daily round of their faithful service: grant, we beseech thee, that many men may be moved by thy Holy Spirit to offer themselves for the ministry, so that the work begun long ago and far away may be continued here and everywhere until the second coming of thy dear Son, in whose name we make these our petitions and thanksgivings.

FIVE PRAYERS FOR ADVENT III

I

Deo gratias agamus pro Sanctae Ecclesiae ministerio.

V. Sic nos existimet homo:
R. Ut ministros Christi et dispensatores mysteriorum
  Dei.   1 *Cor.* 4.1.

Omnipotens sempiterne Deus, cujus Filius benedictus, pontifex omnium hominum indefessus, apud te pro nobis perpetuo interpellat:

Gratias tibi agimus quod usque a die Pentecostes assidue operatur clerus Sanctae tuae Ecclesiae: quod episcopi in dioecesibus suis, presbyteri et diaconi domi et peregre ut pastores gregum laborant; quod interpretes in docendo, in adorando ductores, ministros in diurnis officiis sedulos et fideles se praebent: concede, quaesumus, ut multi a Sancto tuo Spiritu adducti se huic ministerio dedicent, ut opus diu et longe inceptum hic et ubique procedat, donec iterum adveniat Filius tuus dilectus, cujus in nomine orationes has et benedictiones offerimus.

2

Let us pray for the inspiration of the Holy Spirit in the ministry of the Word.

V. Their sound is gone out into all lands:
R. And their words into the ends of the world.

Ps. 19.4.

O Lord God, who at Pentecost didst send the Holy Spirit the Comforter to guide thy servants into all truth, and strengthen them in preaching the gospel of Jesus:

Grant that the Ministry of thy Church may hear his voice today, and faithfully deliver his message: guide them to think rightly, to speak wisely, and bravely to bear witness to the truth as it is in Christ Jesus; so that the problems and difficulties of man's life may be brought into thy counsels, there to be purified and cleansed to an issue of holiness; through

2

Oremus ut per infusionem Sancti Spiritus ministerium Verbi dirigatur.

V. In omnem terram exivit sonus eorum:
R. Et in fines orbis terrae verbum eorum.   *Ps.* 18.5.

Domine Deus, qui die Pentecostes Sanctum Spiritum Paracletum misisti, qui famulos tuos omnem veritatem doceret, et in evangelio Jesu Christi praedicando firmaret:

Concede ut Ecclesiae tuae ministri vocem ejus hoc tempore exaudientes fideliter nuntient; doce, quaesumus, eos cogitare honeste, loqui prudenter, veritati Jesu Christi testimonium fortiter perhibere, ut omnes homines curas diurnas et necessitates suas ita consilio subjiciant tuo, ut ipsa vita sanctificetur; per

3

Let us pray for the faithful use of the sacraments of the Church.

V. He shewed me a pure river of water of life, clear as crystal:
R. Proceeding out of the throne of God and of the Lamb. *Rev.* 22.1.

O God, Creator of the world, who hast ordained that we may learn of the things that are unseen and spiritual through the things that are seen and temporal:

Grant us grace to partake faithfully in the sacraments which thou hast entrusted to the care and use of thy holy Church: especially help us to see in Holy Baptism the sanctification of human life, the building up of thy kingdom, and the dedication of our will to thy service; grant that in the sacrament of the Altar we may worship and glorify thee, and also receive from thee the grace which we need in order that we may live according to thy will; to this end bless, we pray thee, the ministers of thy sacraments, that they may be found faithful stewards of thy mysteries, rightly serving thee and thy people, to thy greater glory and our spiritual advantage; through

3

Oremus ut sacramentis Ecclesiae fideliter utamur.

V. Ostendit mihi fluvium aquae vitae splendidum tamquam crystallum:
R. Procedentem de sede Dei et Agni.   *Apoc.* 22.1.

Deus, Creator mundi, qui nos per ea quae videntur et temporalia sunt ea aeterna quae non videntur discere voluisti:

Da nobis gratiam ut sacramentorum fideles fiamus participes, quae Ecclesiae tuae curanda mandasti; et praecipue ut in Baptismo sacro vitam humanam consecrari, regnum tuum aedificari, nos ipsos tuo servitio dedicari intelligamus; concede ut nos in sacramento Communionis sacrae te adorantes et glorificantes gratiam a te accipiamus qua opus est secundum tuam voluntatem victuris; cujus causa te oramus ut sacramentorum tuorum ministris benedicas, ut mysteriorum fideles dispensatores inveniantur, et tibi et populo tuo ad tuam majorem gloriam et beneficium nostrum recte deserviant; per

4

Let us pray for the pastoral work of the ministry.

V. The Lord is my shepherd:
R. I shall not want. *Ps.* 23.1.

O heavenly Father, who didst send thy Son Jesus Christ to lay down his life that we might have life more abundantly:

Grant that the ministers of thy Church may tend the flocks committed to their charge and care, with heavenly wisdom, unfailing gentleness, and stedfast perseverance and courage; grant that the relationship of the bishop to his diocese, and of every parish priest to his people may conform more and more to the heavenly pattern of thy love revealed to us by the great shepherd of the flocks, Christ Jesus our Saviour; that so both thy ministers and those to whom they minister may become one flock united in the fold of thy Church to thy honour and glory; through the same

4

Oremus pro Sanctae Ecclesiae pastoribus.

V. Dominus regit me;
R. Et nihil mihi deerit. *Ps.* 22.1.

Pater caelestis, cujus Filius Jesus Christus suam animam posuit ut nos vitam abundantius haberemus:

Concede ut Ecclesiae tuae pastores gregibus curae suae commissis ministrantes semper sapientia benignitate fortitudine perseverent; da, quaesumus, ut in dioecesibus episcopi, in parochiis presbyteri magis in dies affectus tui caelestis imitentur exemplum, quod nobis ipse magnus ovium pastor, Jesus Christus Salvator noster, exhibuit; ut et ministri tui et ei quibus ministrant in Sanctae Ecclesiae ovili grex unicus fiant, ad tuum honorem et gloriam; per eundem

5

Let us pray for the ministry of the whole Church to mankind.

V. Ye also as lively stones are built up a spiritual house:

R. To be an holy priesthood.   1 *Pet.* 2.5.

O God, for whose glory and pleasure all things are and were created, and who hast given to man freedom and power to love thee:

We beseech thee to let thy loving mercy rest upon all thy servants, that the work of thy holy Church may be set forward and accomplished, and that all mankind may know thy Name and glorify thee in thy kingdom; may thy Holy Spirit inspire all the members of thy Church, both clergy and laity, to accept the obligations of thy service, and day by day to bear their witness to the message of the Gospel, that all the world may know that there is none other name in which mankind can be saved except the name of Christ Jesus; to whom with thee and the Holy Spirit in all reverence be ascribed glory, dominion and worship, now and for evermore.

5

Oremus ut tota Ecclesia toti humano generi bene ministret.

V. Et ipsi tamquam lapides vivi superaedificamini domus spiritualis:
R. Sacerdotium sanctum. 1 *Pet.* 2.5.

Domine Deus, cujus propter gloriam et voluntatem creata sunt omnia, cujus munere te homines et volunt et possunt diligere:

Concede, quaesumus, ut famuli tui, affectu tuo et misericordia freti, sanctae tuae Ecclesiae opus ita proficiant ut omnes homines nomen tuum agnoscant, et in tuo regno glorificent; oramus ut per Sancti tui Spiritus infusionem omnes, et clerici simul et laici, se tuo servitio libenter subjiciant, et quotidie Evangelio testimonium suum perhibeant, ut sciant omnes homines non aliud esse nomen nisi Jesu Christi in quo homines salvos oporteat fieri; cui tecum et cum Sancto Spiritu sit gloria et potestas et adoratio nunc et in saecula saeculorum.

FOUR PRAYERS FOR ADVENT IV
(Arising from Handel's *Messiah*.)

I. THE HIGHWAY

Let us pray for strength to prepare the way of God in men's hearts.

V. Comfort ye, comfort ye my people, saith your God:
R. Speak ye comfortably to Jerusalem.   *Isa.* 40.1.

O God, who hast made thyself known to us as our God, and wast the God of our fathers before us:
   We beseech thee to reveal thy glory to us and to all mankind, that we may know it as our hope in the way of salvation; give us strength; strength to prepare thy way in life's tangled perplexities; strength to fill up every abyss and gulf in thy pathway; strength to smooth away the hill and the height from before thee; and strength to make the rough places plain and to straighten the crooked; grant that thus labouring we may build a highway for thy entrance to the hearts of all men, that they may abide the day of thy coming with joyful expectation and courage; through him who is himself the way, even thy Son, Christ Jesus our Lord.

FOUR PRAYERS FOR ADVENT IV
(Arising from Handel's *Messiah*.)

I. THE HIGHWAY

Potestatem petamus ut Deo viam in cordibus hominum praeparemus.

V. Consolamini, consolamini, populc meus, dicit Deus vester:
R. Loquimini ad cor Jerusalem.   *Isa.* 40.1.

Domine Deus, qui teipsum Deum nostrum nobis revelavisti, sicut Deus patrum quoque nostrorum fuisti:

Rogamus te ut nobis et hominibus omnibus gloriam tuam facias manifestam, ut eam spem esse nostram sciamus in via salutis; da nobis potestatem ut inter vitae difficultates semitam tibi paremus, ut vallem omnem implere, montem omnem et collem te adveniente possimus humiliare, ut prava in directa, in vias planas aspera faciamus; et denique via tibi in omnium hominum animas muniatur, ut cum spe et fortitudine diem adventus tui exspectent: per eum qui ipse est Via, Filium tuum Jesum Christum, Dominum nostrum.

2. THE GOSPEL

Let us thank God for the Incarnation of Jesus Christ.

V. Behold, a virgin shall conceive, and bear a son:
R. And shall call his name Immanuel, God with us.
Isa. 7.14.

O Lord God, who didst send thy Son our Saviour to take man upon him, that he might bring us the good tidings of thy love:

We thank thee that thou hast dispelled the gross darkness of sin which covered the earth, and the darkness of ignorance; we thank thee that we have been allowed to see the brightness of thy rising, and enabled by thy Holy Spirit to walk in the light of thy glory; we thank thee that the Gospel message has been faithfully proclaimed among us, and the coming of the Saviour made known to Jew and Gentile, to kings and to peoples; grant that all upon whom the rays of thy glorious light shall be seen may rise and come to thee in joy and thanksgiving: through Jesus our Emmanuel, thy blessed Son.

2. THE GOSPEL

Deo gratias agamus pro Incarnatione Jesu Christi.

V. Ecce, virgo concipiet et pariet filium:
R. Et vocabitur nomen ejus Emmanuel.   *Isa.* 7.14.

Domine Deus, qui Filium tuum Salvatorem nostrum misisti, ut hominem assumeret, et nobis affectum tuum evangelizaret:

Tibi gratias agimus, quod caliginem quae gentes operiebat et tenebras ignorantiae dispersisti; quod per Sanctum tuum Spiritum nobis licuit splendorem ortus tui videre, et in lumine tuae gloriae ambulare; tibi benedicimus quia evangelium inter nos ita fideliter est praedicatum ut Salvatoris adventus Judaeis et gentibus, regibus et populis sit nuntiatus; concede ut surgant omnes quibus lucis tuae radii orientur, et ad te cum gratiarum actione et gaudio appropinquent; per Emmanuel nostrum, Filium tuum benedictum Jesum Christum.

3. THE LIGHT

Let us pray for grace to know Christ as the Light of the World.

V. The people that walked in darkness have seen a great light:
R. And they that dwell in the land of the shadow of death, upon them hath the light shined.   *Isa.* 9.2.

O God, Almighty, Everloving, Holy Father, in whose dear Son's coming we thankfully rejoice at this season:

Grant, we beseech thee, that we may be allowed to know him truly as the light of the world, and to receive from him the good gifts which we need in our conflict with evil: may his grace inspire us; his wisdom guide us; his power enable us; his love encourage us; and his peace ever dwell with us; may the land of the shadow of death in which for a while we dwell as sojourners and pilgrims become to us the fringes and frontiers of the heavenly country, where there await those who love thee to the end rest eternal and perpetual light; through him who is the light that lighteth every man, Jesus Christ, thy Son, our Lord.

3. THE LIGHT

Gratiam rogemus ut Jesum Christum mundi lucem agnoscamus.

V. Populus qui ambulabat in tenebris vidit lucem magnam:
R. Habitantibus in regione umbrae mortis, lux orta est eis. *Isa.* 9.2.

Deus Omnipotens, Pater sanctissime, cujus Filii adventum hoc tempore celebramus gaudentes:

Concede, quaesumus, ut nobis liceat eum mundi lucem agnoscere, ut ab eo bona accipiamus, quibus opus est nobis contra malum pugnantibus: da ut nos gratia ejus inspiret, sapientia dirigat, potestas confortet, amor impellat, pax comitetur; et regio umbrae mortis, in qua sicut advenae et peregrini aliquamdiu habitamus, caelestis patriae fiat confinium, ubi eis qui te diligunt quies aeterna et lux perpetua comparantur; per eum qui vera lux est quae omnem hominem illuminat, Jesum Christum Dominum nostrum.

4. THE SHEPHERD

Let us pray that all men may share in the blessings of the Incarnation.

V. There were in the same country shepherds abiding in the field:
R. Keeping watch over their flock by night.

Luke 2.8.

O God, who didst send thine angel to the waking shepherds in the field with the first message of Christ's birth, and didst thereafter allow them to hear the praises of the heavenly multitude:

Grant to us that at this time we may join in the proclamation of thy glory in the highest heaven, and share in thy peace upon earth and good will among men. Open the eyes which are blinded by greed, that they may see the true riches of thy love; unstop the ears which are deafened by the clamour of the world, that they may hear the voice of thy Spirit; set free the limbs that are fettered by sin, that they may be exercised in thy service; give utterance to the tongues that are dumb in ignorance, that they may show forth thy praises. Make thyself known, O Lord, as the great shepherd of the flocks, gather the lambs in thine arms and carry them in thy bosom; feed thy flocks in a green pasture, and lead us forth beside waters of comfort, where it is joy to obey thee, and to serve thee is our peace; through the Babe of Bethlehem, thy Son our Lord.

4. THE SHEPHERD

Oremus ut beneficia Incarnationis omnibus hominibus communicentur.

V. Et pastores erant in regione eadem vigilantes:
R. Et custodientes vigilias noctis super gregem suum.
Luc. 2.8.

Domine Deus, qui pastoribus in agro vigilantibus angelum tuum misisti, qui primus Christum esse natum annuntiaret, et eis concessisti ut caelestis multitudinis laudes audirent:

Praesta ut nos quoque hoc tempore gloriam tuam in altissimis praedicemus, et tuae in terra pacis et bonae inter homines voluntatis fiamus participes. Aperi, quaesumus, oculos eorum qui propter avaritiam obcaecantur, ut affectus tui veras divitias videant; aures acue quae mundi clamoribus obtunduntur, ut Sancti Spiritus tui vocem percipiant; membra solve quae peccatorum vinculis alligantur, ut exerceantur in obsequio tuo; libera linguas quae propter ignorantiam obmutuerunt, ut laudes tuas annuntient. Ostende teipsum, Domine, magnum gregum pastorem, agnos in tuo brachio congrega, et in sinu tuo extolle, oves pasce tuos in loco pascuae et educa super aquam refectionis, ut obsequendo tibi gaudeamus et in servitio tuo pacem inveniamus; per Infantem in Bethlehem natum, Filium tuum Dominum nostrum.

FOUR PRAYERS FOR THE NEW YEAR

1. THANKSGIVING

Let us thank God for the blessings bestowed on us during the past year.

V. O give thanks unto the Lord, for he is gracious:
R. And his mercy endureth for ever.   *Ps.* 107.1.

O Lord God, heavenly Father, of whom cometh all that is good and to whom we look for succour and safety:

We thank thee for the love which has watched over us through the past year, for the temporal welfare with which thou hast blessed us, for the protection with which thy grace has shielded us in times of spiritual danger, and enabled us to stand firm in face of temptation: we thank thee for the growth of our knowledge of thee, O Father, and of Jesus Christ thy Son our Saviour, and of the Holy Spirit the Comforter: give us grace to be ready according to thy will to receive the daily continuance of these thy great mercies; through

FOUR PRAYERS FOR THE NEW YEAR

1. THANKSGIVING

Deo gratias agamus ob beneficia quae nobis per praeteritum hunc annum largitus est.

V. Confitemini Domino quoniam bonus:
R. Quoniam in saeculum misericordia ejus.

Ps. 106.1.

Domine Deus, Pater caelestis, a quo bona cuncta procedunt, cujus gratia salutem et auxilium exspectamus:

Tibi gratias agimus pro caritate qua nos per praeteritum hunc annum custodivisti, pro temporalibus bonis omnibus quibus nos adauxisti, pro tutamine quo animas ita in periculis defendisti ut contra tentationem stare possimus: benedicimus tibi quia te, O Pater, et Jesum Christum Filium tuum Salvatorem et Sanctum Spiritum Paracletum melius nosse didicimus: da nobis gratiam, quaesumus, ut secundum voluntatem tuam haec tua beneficia quotidie percipere valeamus; per

2. ASPIRATION

Let us pray for a Christian frame of mind in the New Year.

V. O satisfy us with thy mercy and that soon:
R. So shall we rejoice and be glad all the days of our life. *Ps.* 90.14.

O God, from whom alone all creation draws life and power and will:

As we stand at the beginning of another year we lift up our hearts to thee in praise and thanksgiving; we praise thee for the majesty of thy glory, for the mightiness of thy power, for thy perfection of purpose; for all that is thine, angels who do thee service, saints departed in thy faith and fear, thy servants still at war with evil here on earth, we praise thy holy Name, and long to be counted amongst those who are incorporate in the Body of thy dear Son, and in him are thine: give us grace to live through the New Year as thy loving servants, resisting evil, following after goodness, looking forward to eternal life in thy kingdom; through

2. ASPIRATION

Oremus ut per annum nunc incipientem Christianum vere animum induamus.

V. Repleti sumus mane misericordia tua:
R. Et exsultavimus et delectati sumus omnibus diebus nostris. *Ps.* 89.14.

Domine Deus, a quo vitam, vires, voluntatem omnis accipit creatura:

Nos novum ineuntes annum cum laude et benedictione ad te sursum corda levamus; te pro gloriae tuae majestate, pro potestatis magnitudine, pro voluntatis tuae perfectione laudamus; nos recordati quodcumque tuum est, angelos qui tibi ministrant, sanctos omnes qui in fide et timore tui defuncti sunt, famulos qui etiam nunc in terra contra malitiam proeliantur, sancto tuo benedicimus nomini, et inter eos numerari desideramus qui in Filio tuo dilecto tui sunt facti, in corpore ejus incorporati: da nobis gratiam ut per novum annum sicut pii tui famuli malo resistamus, sequamur bonum, aeternam vitam in regno tuo anticipemus; per

3. SINS AGAINST GOD

Let us pray for pardon for our sins against God.

V. Have mercy upon me, O God, after thy great goodness:
R. According to the multitude of thy mercies do away mine offences. *Ps.* 51.1.

O God, to whom no sinner turns in vain for pardon, and with whom there is an ever-flowing fountain of mercy:

Have pity, we humbly beseech thee, upon us who look back with grief upon our many sins against thy Majesty during the past year: we confess that we have done amiss in many times forgetting thee, and many times disobeying thy commandments: our worship has often been unreflecting and thoughtless; our prayers, words without meaning; our praise, scanty and careless: we have not always given thee thanks for thy blessings, nor trusted thee in all times of trial and danger: for these and all other our offences we humbly beg for forgiveness and for grace of amendment; through

3. SINS AGAINST GOD

Oremus ut remittantur quaecumque in Deum peccavimus.

V. Miserere mei, Deus, secundum magnam misericordiam tuam:
R. Et secundum multitudinem miserationum tuarum
    dele iniquitatem meam. *Ps.* 50.1.

Domine Deus, quem nemo inane indulgentiam rogat, in quo fontem misericordiae perennem habemus:

Miserere, quaesumus, nostri, qui multa per praeteritum annum in te peccata contristati respicimus; confitemur quod inique fecimus saepe tui obliti, saepe mandatorum tuorum contraria facientes: nullam in te adorando curam habuimus, in precando nullam intentionem, nullam copiam in laudando; nec satis tibi pro beneficiis tuis gratias egimus, nec tibi soli in probationibus et periculis sumus confisi: pro his et aliis omnibus peccatis nostris indulgentiam et poenitentiae gratiam humiliter obsecramus; per

4. SINS AGAINST OUR NEIGHBOUR

Let us pray for pardon for our sins against our neighbour.

V. Thou shalt love thy neighbour:
R. As thyself. *Matt.* 22.39.

O Almighty God, Ancient of Days, who dwellest in eternal majesty and yet regardest and lovest each of thy children:

Forgive us, for the love of thy dear Son, the many sins which we have committed against our neighbour during the year which is ended; the sins of unfaithful thought and base purpose; the sins of uncharitable deeds and unkindly actions: the sins of unprofitable words and deliberate untruthfulness: by all which our lives have been stained and degraded: and, we beseech thee, give us with thy pardon grace also to amend our ways and serve thee better in the new year of our warfare; through

4. SINS AGAINST OUR NEIGHBOUR

Oremus ut remittantur quaecumque in proximum peccavimus.

V. Diliges proximum tuum:
R. Sicut teipsum. *Matt.* 22.39.

Deus omnipotens, Antique Dierum, qui in majestate sempiterna inhabitas, et tamen filiorum tuorum unumquemque curas et diligis:

Remitte, quaesumus, per Filii tui dilecti affectum ea multa quae in proximos per praeteritum annum peccavimus; quia nos in cogitando turpes et infideles, malignos et invidos in agendo, in loquendo vanos praebuimus et mendaces, quibus omnibus infecta est vita nostra et inquinata: et super remissionem tuam, obsecramus, gratiam nobis concede, ut moribus emendatis per novum annum proeliantes tibi intentius serviamus; per

EPIPHANY
The Spiritual Works of Christian Mercy

1. TEACHING THE IGNORANT

Let us pray for grace to teach the ignorant.

V. When thy word goeth forth:
R. It giveth light and understanding unto the simple.
Ps. 119.130.

O Lord God, who because man cannot know thee by his own wisdom hast graciously revealed thyself through the incarnation of thy Son:
  Grant that thy holy Church may always be eager to teach those who know thee not, and to lead them with the authority of the Holy Spirit to a saving knowledge of the truth as it is in Christ Jesus; through the same

2. COUNSELLING THE DOUBTFUL

Let us pray for grace to counsel the doubtful.

V. If any lack wisdom, let him ask of God:
R. But let him ask in faith, nothing wavering.
Jas. 1.5-6.

O Lord God, whose Son proclaimed a blessing on those who not having seen him have yet believed on him:
  We beseech thee to give us wisdom so to understand the doubts of those who question the truth of

EPIPHANY
The Spiritual Works of Christian Mercy
1. TEACHING THE IGNORANT

Gratiam rogemus ut eos doceamus qui Deum ignorant.

V. Declaratio sermonum tuorum illuminat:
R. Et intellectum dat parvulis. *Ps.* 118.130.

Domine Deus, qui quoniam te homines sua ipsorum sapientia nosse non possunt, per incarnationem Filii tui teipsum nobis propitius revelasti:

Praesta ut ecclesia tua studeat eos qui te ignorant semper docere, et per Sancti Spiritus auctoritatem ad salutarem veri scientiam in Christo Jesu manifestati perducere; per eundem

2. COUNSELLING THE DOUBTFUL

Gratiam rogemus ut consilium dubitantibus demus.

V. Si quis indiget sapientia, postulet a Deo:
R. Postulet autem in fide, nihil haesitans.

Jac. 1.5-6.

Domine Deus, cujus Filius beatos esse dixit eos qui se non vidissent, et in se tamen crederent:

Obsecramus te ut nobis des sapientiam ut cogita-

thy Son's Incarnation, that we may be enabled by thy Holy Spirit to reassure those who hesitate, to relieve those who are in perplexity, and to free the bewildered from their anxiety; through the same

3. ADMONISHING SINNERS

Let us pray for grace to admonish sinners.

V. Then will I teach transgressors thy ways:
R. And sinners shall be converted unto thee.
Ps. 51.13.

O God, whose Son bade sinners turn from their evil ways and repent them and follow him:

Grant, we humbly beseech thee, to thy servants that in true humbleness of heart we may awaken sinners to the hurtfulness of their sin, and help them to follow after that which is right, so that in repentance and faith they and we may hearken to his teaching and try to do his will; who liveth

4. COMFORTING THE AFFLICTED

Let us pray for grace to comfort the afflicted.

V. Comfort yourselves together:
R. And edify one another.   1 *Thess.* 5.11.

O Lord God, to whom troubled souls cry for help in their anguish:

tiones eorum intelligamus qui in veritatem incarnationis Filii tui credere nolunt, et per Sanctum tuum Spiritum certos facere dubitantes, exonerare incertos, anxios cura liberare possimus: per eundem

3. ADMONISHING SINNERS

Gratiam rogemus ut peccatores admoneamus.

V. Docebo iniquos vias tuas:
R. Et impii ad te convertentur.   *Ps.* 50.13.

Domine Deus, cujus Filius peccatores admonere solebat, ut a malo conversi poenitentiam agerent et se sequerentur:

Praesta, quaesumus, famulis tuis ut cum vera humilitate possimus peccatores de nocentia peccati arguere, et ita adjuvare ut quod rectum est adsequantur, ut una cum eis poenitenter et fideliter doctrinam ejus percipere et voluntati ejus obedire conemur; qui tecum

4. COMFORTING THE AFFLICTED

Gratiam rogemus ut miseros consolemur.

V. Consolamini invicem:
R. Et aedificate alterutrum.   1 *Thess.* 5.11.

Domine Deus, quem contristatae hominum animae auxilium in tribulatione implorant:

We beseech thee, give thy servants the grace of devotion and thoughtfulness that in thy name we may cheerfully minister deliverance to the afflicted, consolation to them that are heavy of heart, and to the weary refreshment in the name of the Saviour; through the same

5. PARDONING OFFENDERS

V. Forgive, if ye have aught against any:
R. That your Father also may forgive you your trespasses. *Mark* 11.25.

Eternal and everlasting God, whose blessed Son forgave the soldiers who nailed him to the Cross:

Give us grace never to harbour resentment and thoughts of revenge in our hearts, but always freely to forgive those who offend us or do us harm, as our trust is that thou dost forgive us our offences against thee; through

6. SUCCOURING THE WEAK

V. Strengthen ye the weak hands:
R. And confirm the feeble knees. *Isa.* 35.3.

O Everlasting and Eternal God, by whose power creation is upheld, and who alone art without weakness or faltering:

Assist the frailty of thy servants with the grace of

Concede, quaesumus, famulis tuis bonitatis et mansuetudinis gratiam, ut liberationem oppressis, solacium miseris, refectionem languentibus in nomine Salvatoris libenter suppeditemus; per eundem

5. PARDONING OFFENDERS

V. Dimittite si quid habetis adversus aliquem:

R. Ut et Pater vester dimittat vobis peccata.

Marc. 11.25.

Sempiterne Deus, cujus Filius benedictus militibus dimisit a quibus cruci affigebatur:

Da nobis gratiam ne unquam in animis ultionem et iracundiam foveamus, sed ut velimus semper eis qui nobis adversantur vel nocent dimittere, sicut teipsum nobis in te peccata dimissurum esse confidimus; per

6. SUCCOURING THE WEAK

V. Confortate manus dissolutas:
R. Et genua debilia roborate. *Isa.* 35.3.

Sempiterne Deus, qui omnem sustines creaturam, qui solus neque infirmus neque potes esse inconstans:

thy strength, that we may succour the dejected in spirit, invigorate the feeble in resolution, and revive those who are exhausted in their fight against evil; through

7. PRAYING FOR ALL MEN

V. Pray one for another, that ye may be healed:
R. The fervent prayer of a righteous man availeth much. *Jas.* 5.16.

O God, to whom we have been taught to pray as to our heavenly Father:

Grant us, we beseech thee, such love towards thee that we may see all men as thy children, and rejoice that thy fatherly care is over all the nations of the earth: give us grace to pray for the needs of all, and in the fellowship of our prayer to strengthen the brotherhood which binds us in one communion of service; through

Adjuva, quaesumus, famulos tuos firmitatis gratia tuae, ut contritis corde mederi, haesitantes corroborare, et eos qui contra malitiam proeliantes deficiunt vivificare possimus; per

7. PRAYING FOR ALL MEN

V. Orate pro invicem ut salvemini:
R. Multum valet deprecatio justi assidua. *Jac.* 5.16.

Domine Deus, cui sicut Patri nostro caelesti orare didicimus:

Da nobis, quaesumus, tantum amoris tui affectum, ut omnes homines sicut tuos filios agnoscamus, et gaudeamus te omnes terrae gentes paterna cura protegere: gratiam nobis concede, ut tibi pro omnium necessitatibus faciamus orationes, et in earum communitate fraternum augeamus affectum, quo omnes invicem in tua servitute conjungimur; per

LITTLE LENT
Faith, Hope, and Charity

SEPTUAGESIMA: FAITH

V. Who is he that overcometh the world:
R. But he that believeth that Jesus is the Son of God?
1 John 5.5.

O Lord God, maker of heaven and earth, and of the sea and of all that in them is:

Establish in us, we beseech thee, the faith without which we cannot see the working of thy hand today in the life of mankind; grant that we may put our trust in thee only, and rely upon thy might and protection for the triumph of good over evil: help us to answer thy call to work for thy kingdom, and in spite of disappointments and failures to be certain of victory; through

SEXAGESIMA: HOPE

V. We have fled for refuge to lay hold of the hope set before us:
R. Which we have as an anchor of the soul.
Heb. 6.18.

O God Almighty, whose dear Son taught his disciples to look forward with hope to life everlasting:

Grant that we may set our hope on thy mercy: pity our weakness; accept our repentance; pardon

LITTLE LENT
Faith, Hope, and Charity

SEPTUAGESIMA: FAITH

V. Quis est qui vincit mundum:
R. Nisi qui credit quoniam Jesus est Filius Dei?

1 Joan. 5.5.

Domine Deus, qui caelum et terram et mare et quae sunt in eis omnia creavisti:

Confirma, quaesumus, in nobis eam fidem sine qua non possumus tuam rerum humanarum gubernationem agnoscere; praesta ut te solo confisi, et tutela tua et potentia freti, in bono malum vincere valeamus; adjuva nos ut secundum mandata tua laboremus in regni tui adventum, et quamvis dejecti saepe et deficientes victoriam confidenter anticipemus; per

SEXAGESIMA: HOPE

V. Confugimus ad tenendam propositam spem:
R. Quam sicut anchoram habemus animae.

Heb. 6.18.

Omnipotens Deus, cujus Filius dilectus discipulis suis aeternae spem vitae praecipiebat:

Praesta ut misericordiae tuae spem habeamus; infirmitatem nostram condona, poenitentiam specta,

our wickedness; and grant that at the last day we may not be shut out of thy kingdom, but may in company with the saints who have gone before us be granted the clear sight of thy glory, and enjoy for ever the abundant victory won by thy love; through the same

QUINQUAGESIMA: CHARITY

V. Now abideth faith, hope, and charity:
R. But the greatest of these is charity.   1 *Cor.* 13.13.

O God, heavenly Father, whose every motion towards us springs from thine inexhaustible love:

Enable us, we humbly beseech thee, cheerfully to sacrifice ourselves for the well-being of those with whom we have to do, and also to love them with the tender love which thou hast for the world, that so though now we see thee darkly through the veil of our blindness, we with them may presently see thee in the fulness of light; through

peccatis ignosce; da nobis ut in extremo die includamur in regno tuo caelesti, et una cum sanctis omnibus qui ante nos antecesserunt gloriam tuam aperte intueamur, et semper victoriae fructum tuo partae affectu percipiamus; per eundem

QUINQUAGESIMA: CHARITY

V. Nunc autem manent fides, spes, caritas:
R. Major autem horum est caritas.   1 *Cor.* 13.13.

Domine Deus, Pater caelestis, qui nos semper inexplebili tuo amoris affectu inspiras:

Praesta, quaesumus, ut nos nostri ipsorum obliti ultro eis inter quos versamur prodesse, et eadem eos caritate qua tu ipse diligere studeamus; ut, quamvis caecitate nostra offuscati te nunc in aenigmate videamus, aliquando cum eis facie ad faciem te contemplari possimus; per

THREE PRAYERS FOR TRINITY

1

Let us pray for the grace of obedience.

V. Blessed is the man that feareth the Lord:
R. He hath great delight in his commandments.

Ps. 112.1.

O God, Sovereign Lord, to whom allegiance and service are to be rendered:
 Grant that, as the life of true faith is manifested in works of pure righteousness, we may gladly yield ourselves and our doings to the guidance of thy kingly direction; through

2

Let us pray that we may love God rightly.

V. Thou shalt love the Lord thy God:
R. With all thy heart, and with all thy soul, and with all thy mind, and with all thy strength.

Mark 12.30.

O God, author of all that is, whom surely to know and truly to love is man's perfect happiness:
 Grant that all those who know thee may learn how to love thee; through

THREE PRAYERS FOR TRINITY

1

Oremus ut obedientiae gratia induamur.

V. Beatus vir qui timet Dominum:
R. In mandatis ejus volet nimis. *Ps.* 111.1.

Domine Deus, cui fidem et obsequium praestare debemus: Concede ut, quoniam vera fides in operibus justitiae demonstratur, nosmet ipsos et opera nostra tibi regi et gubernatori laeti subjiciamus: per

2

Oremus ut Deum recte diligamus.

V. Diliges Dominum Deum tuum:
R. Ex toto corde tuo, et ex tota anima tua, et ex tota mente tua et ex tota virtute tua. *Marc.* 12.30

Deus, qui omnia quae sunt creavisti, quem vere nosse et vere diligere est hominibus summa beatitudo:

Praesta ut omnes qui te noverunt te discant diligere; per

3

Let us pray for grace to love our neighbour.

V. Thou shalt love thy neighbour:
R. As thyself. *Mark* 12.31.

O God, Lord of all judgement, who hast taught us that man's love of himself is the rule of his love for his neighbour:

Grant that we doubt not our life to be of so great a price that in loving our neighbour as thou hast taught us we may truly fulfil thy commandment; through

3

Gratiam rogemus ut proximum diligamus.

V. Diliges proximum tuum:
R. Tamquam teipsum. *Marc.* 12.31.

Deus, omnium hominum Judex, qui nos docuisti hominem sicut se ipsum debere proximum suum diligere:

Concede ut certe sciamus vitam nostram ita esse pretiosam, ut in proximis diligendis mandatum tuum vere perficiamus, per

Appendixes

APPENDIX 1

THE CURSUS IN LATIN AND ENGLISH

The Latin versions of the prayers in this book have been written to accord with the rules of the Latin Cursus. It was Canon Wallis who first introduced me to the admirable account by the late Professor A. C. Clark of *The Cursus in Mediaeval and Vulgar Latin* (O.U.P., 1910), which is the main source of information and illustration in the following notes.

Study of the Gregorian Sacramentary and other collections of early and medieval Latin prayers reveals that their authors observed certain rules of composition, whereby the clauses and sentences were made to end in definite rhythmic patterns. These are comparable to the well-known *clausulae* of Ciceronian Latin prose, but with the difference that the rhythms are based no longer on quantity but on accent. The three favourite *clausulae* of Cicero were shown by Zielinski to be built from different combinations of the two metrical feet, the cretic (— ⌣ —) and the trochee (— ⌣), as follows:

1. — ⌣ — | — ⌣

     e.g. pācĕ fīrmāvĭt.

2. — ⏑ — | — ⏑ ≃

        e.g. cēssĭt aūdācĭă.

3. — ⏑ — | — ⏑ | — ≃

        e.g. cōpĭām cōmpărāvĭt.

When at the end of the fourth century accent began to supplant quantity, these three types persisted in the liturgical and official documents of the Christian Church as favourite endings, though based on the normal accents of ordinary speech.

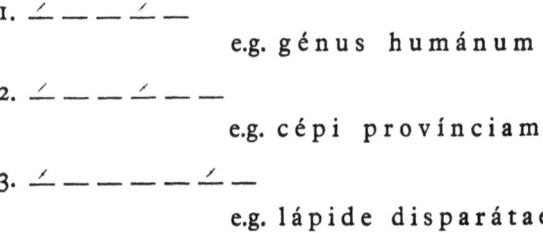

1. ´ — — ´ —

        e.g. génus humánum

2. ´ — — ´ — —

        e.g. cépi província m

3. ´ — — — — ´ —

        e.g. lápide disparátae

The first of these became known as *cursus planus*, the second as *cursus tardus*, the third as *cursus velox*.

The rule is that an accent on the penultimate syllable requires another accent on either the 5th or the 7th syllable from the end,

```
e.g. Chrístum misísti      (planus)
         5   4      3 2  1
   or laéti accipiámus     (velox)
       7  6 5   4 32  1
```

If there is an accent on the antepenultimate syllable, another accent is required on the 6th syllable from the end,

e.g. nóbis descríberent   (*tardus*)
    6 5   4   3 2 1

  possímus elígere   (*tardus*)
   7 6 5   4 3 2 1

The influence of the Cursus is also clearly traceable in the English of the Book of Common Prayer. It was natural, in fact inevitable, for Canon Wallis, deeply imbued as he was with the thought and language of our English Liturgy, to shape his own prayers in harmony with the rhythms and structures which he could observe in it. I quote from one of his letters:

"Our Reformers were familiar with the Cursus, and took it over into the English of the Book of Common Prayer. In the Sunday Collects, for instance, there are 80 examples of the Cursus in the course of 148 clause-endings. Most of the remainder end with an accented syllable, e.g. 'armour of light', 'ruler and guide', giving the scheme ´ _ _ ´
                    4 3 2 1

"Do you agree that this shows a feeling after a cursus-ending rather like the Latin, but adapted to a language rich in monosyllables? It seems to me to be clear from e.g. the first Collect in the Communion Service, 'from whom no sécrets are híd'. Here is a

deliberate refraining from using the *planus* 'from whom no sécrets are hídden'."

Canon Wallis summed it all up in a working rule that there must be not fewer than two unaccented syllables before the last accented syllable of a clause or sentence.

But after all, it is "the spirit that giveth life", and it will not be for academic details of style and structure that its users will mainly value this "attempt to marshal the occurring thoughts of a Christian man into a body of Christian prayer, cast into the formal rhythms which confer dignity, and sometimes even give a deeper meaning to the expressions used".

F.C.G.

APPENDIX 2

TRADITIONAL ENDINGS OF COLLECTS

For considerations of space and convenience the usual endings to the individual prayers have been omitted in the text, except for such bare indications as "through", "per", and the like. The traditional endings, in English and Latin, to cover all variations are given below. There are several medieval mnemonics giving a summary of the scheme, of which the following is a specimen:

"Per Dominum" dicas, si Patrem Presbyter oras.
Si Christum memores, "per eundem" dicere debes.
Si loqueris Christo, "qui vivis" scire memento;
"Qui tecum", si sit collectae finis in ipso.
Si memores Flamen, "ejusdem" dic prope finem.

PRAYERS ADDRESSED TO GOD THE FATHER

through. Through Jesus Christ thy Son our Lord, who liveth and reigneth with thee in the unity of the Holy Spirit, ever one God, world without end.

per. Per Dominum nostrum Jesum Christum Filium tuum, qui tecum vivit et regnat in unitate Spiritus Sancti, Deus per omnia saecula saeculorum.

through the same. Through the same thy Son Jesus Christ our Lord, who liveth and reigneth with thee in the unity of the Holy Spirit, ever one God, world without end.

per eundem. Per eundem Dominum nostrum Jesum Christum Filium tuum, qui tecum vivit et regnat in unitate Spiritus Sancti, Deus per omnia saecula saeculorum.

who liveth. Who liveth and reigneth with thee in the unity of the Holy Spirit, ever one God, world without end. (*or* in the unity of the same Spirit)

qui tecum. Qui tecum vivit et regnat in unitate Spiritus Sancti, Deus per omnia saecula saeculorum. (*or* in unitate ejusdem Spiritus Sancti)

PRAYERS ADDRESSED TO GOD THE SON

who livest. Who livest and reignest with the Father, in the unity of the Holy Spirit, ever one God, world without end.

qui vivis. Qui vivis et regnas cum Deo Patre, in unitate Spiritus Sancti, Deus per omnia saecula saeculorum.

who with. Who with the Father and the same Holy Spirit livest and reignest, ever one God, world without end.

qui cum Patre. Qui cum Patre et eodem Spiritu Sancto vivis et regnas, Deus per omnia saecula saeculorum.

PRAYERS ADDRESSED TO THE TRINITY

Who livest and reignest, ever one God, world without end.

Qui vivis et regnas Deus per omnia saecula saeculorum.

www.ingramcontent.com/pod-product-compliance
Lightning Source LLC
Chambersburg PA
CBHW071436160426
43195CB00013B/1924